MW01234212

TESTIMONIALS FOR KENNY YOUMANS

Kenny Youmans has the gift of finding the silver lining in all life experiences. In this day and age of confrontation and dispute, there is someone who sees the good side of people and their legacies left behind. Kenny does extensive research on his subject and brings out the best of "the rest of the story." He has the gift of capturing what most of the world doesn't know and presenting it in the most enjoyable way.

—Glenda Maxwell Bell, past president, Mountain
Findings, Highlands, North Carolina

Kenny Youmans has compiled a number of essays he has written into a book that I highly recommend. He has written about great American traditions and events that are entertaining and serve to remind us of the great privilege we have to live in America.

—Joe Spence, past president, Russell
Reynolds Associates, Atlanta, Georgia

Kenny Youmans's writings can evoke many reactions in the reader. His stories can be either inspirational, challenging, humorous, thought provoking, informative, or just plain enjoyable. Any one of his stories can be honorably defined by one or more of these adjectives. The only thing better than hearing Kenny tell a story is to be privileged to read one of his written works. Indeed, Kenny Youmans is a master storyteller.

—Lorraine Bryant, Highlands, North Carolina

Kenny Youmans has a unique gift of conveying historic moments as if they are happening in real time. Kenny is one of the most captivating storytellers and writers I have had the pleasure of hearing and reading. This book will provide the reader with an opportunity to engage with some of the most inspirational moments in history as only Kenny can deliver.

—Jerry Moore, cofounder, Main Street Payments, Highlands, North Carolina

I have been enjoying the "Life on the Sunny Side" articles written by Kenny Youmans for the Highlands, North Carolina, newspaper for several years and have always found them to be well written and flowing with both interesting and factual information about a wide range of topics appealing to everyone. Whether they discuss background on important dates or individuals in our US history; ordinary people from all walks of life who were instrumental in forming our well-known, special days of recognition; holiday traditions; special songs; or entertainers we grew up watching in the early days of television and the booming movie industry, they are always enjoyable and often full of interesting information we have forgotten or were never aware of. I will be looking forward to both the book compilation of some of Kenny's previous articles I have missed as well as future articles in *Highlands Newspaper* over the coming years.

—Pat Summerell Ramsey, Savannah, Georgia

I am one of the biggest fans of the articles written by Kenny Youmans over the years that I have known him. Particularly appealing to me has been the diversity of content—humorous articles concerning popular individuals not known by many to historic articles giving the backstories on famous events as well as interesting information on songs and how they were written. It was more than obvious that he has done his homework, as there has always been a highly reliable degree of accuracy of fact. He often opens with a "hook" that grabs your attention early and then walks you through a wonderland of interesting stories and wraps up with an amazing conclusion. He will, from time to time, quote Paul Harvey's "and now you know the rest of the story." I have saved several of my favorite Kenny Youmans articles to use in some of my teaching lessons and in a few presentations (speeches) I have given in the last few years. I consider them really good stuff and very worthy of retaining for future fans to enjoy.

—Stewart Hall Jr., past president, Hughes
Supply, Inc., Orlando, Florida

On many occasions, I have had the distinct pleasure of hearing my friend Kenny Youmans speak to civic and other religious groups like the Rotary Club and Sunday School classes on subjects varying from humor to history and with a unique appreciation of his southern heritage of gentlemanly kindness. Hearing Kenny speak and tell his interesting and entertaining stories is always a special and valued opportunity, as he is a master raconteur. Over the past several years, Kenny has gathered his stories together and is now offering them in printed form. His stories are educational, enjoyable, and entertaining. He presents them in a friendly and folksy style that leaves you with a warmth in your heart and a smile on your face. He has been a friend for more than forty years, and I am so pleased that his stories are being offered to a wider audience.

—Raleigh (Sandy) Seay Jr., PhD, Seay Management Consultants, Inc.

Kenny Youmans's articles will make you smile and always bless your heart.

—Mandy Reames, Highlands, North Carolina

Kenny Youmans is a modern-day Will Rogers. He inspires you and also makes you laugh. He is very entertaining. His message is a reminder of what life is all about.

—Corb Hankey, CEO, Fairfax Properties, Inc.

I call Kenny's message "a touch of life." He has a way of bringing everyday occurrences into what life is all about. It's really the things that make life so special. He knows and shares that.

—Robert Fechner, former vice president of
EF Hutton, Winter Park, Florida

THE SUNNY SIDE OF LIFE

The Sunny Side of Life

KENNY YOUMANS

Charleston, SC
www.PalmettoPublishing.com

The Sunny Side of Life

Copyright © 2022 by Kenny Youmans

All rights reserved

No portion of this book may be reproduced, stored in a retrieval
system, or transmitted in any form by any means–electronic,
mechanical, photocopy, recording, or other–except for brief
quotations in printed reviews, without prior permission of the author.

First Edition

Hardcover ISBN: 979-8-8229-0046-2

Paperback ISBN: 979-8-88590-889-4

You can't help someone climb the ladder of success without getting a little closer to the top yourself.

—Kenny Youmans

CONTENTS

POEMS AND QUOTES

"Dreams"

Hold fast to dreams

For if dreams die

Life is a broken-winged bird

That cannot fly.

Hold fast to dreams

For when dreams go

Life is a barren field

Frozen with snow.[1]

—Langston Hughes, from *The Collected Works of Langston Hughes*

1   Hughes, Langston. "Dreams." Poets.org. Accessed August 28, 2022. https://www.poets.org/poems/dreams.

When things go wrong, as they sometimes will,

when the road you're trudging seems all uphill

when the funds are low and the debts are high,

and you want to smile but you have to sigh,

when care is pressing you down a bit - rest
if you must, but don't you quit

Success is failure turned inside out, The
silver tint of clouds of doubt

And you can never tell how close you are,
It may be near, when it seems afar

So, stick to the fight when you are hardest hit, It's
when things seem worst that you mustn't quit.[2]

—Edgar Albert Guest

---

2   Guest, Edgar A. "Don't Quit." Poemanalysis.com. Accessed August 28, 2022.
https://www.poemanalysis.com/edgar-guest/dont-quit/.

Nothing in this world can take the place of persistence, Talent will not; Nothing is more common than unsuccessful men with talent. Genius will not; Unrewarded genius is almost a proverb. Education will not; The world is full of educated derelicts. Persistence and determination alone are omnipotent. The slogan "Press On!" has solved and always will solve the problems of the human race.

—Calvin Coolidge (1872–1933)

KEEP ON THE SUNNY SIDE

Keep on the Sunny Side

Always on the Sunny Side

Keep on the Sunny Side of life

It will help us every day

It will brighten all the way

If we keep on the Sunny Side of life[3]

IN 1899 ADA BLENKHORN was inspired by her nephew to write this Christian hymn. Blenkhorn's nephew was disabled and always wanted his wheelchair pushed down the sunny side of the street. The Carter Family learned of the song from A. P. Carter's uncle, who was a music teacher, and they recorded the song in Camden, New Jersey, in 1928. "Keep on the Sunny Side" became their theme song on the radio in later years. A. P. Carter's tombstone has a gold record of the song embedded in it.

---

3   Wikipedia. "Keep on the Sunny Side." Wikipedia.org. Accessed August 28, 2022.
https://www.en.wikipedia.org/wiki/Keep_on_the_Sunny_Side#lyrics.

In later years, the Carter Family treated "Keep on the Sunny Side" as a theme song. A 1964 album by the Carter Family (with special guest vocalist Johnny Cash) was titled *Keep on the Sunny Side*, and Cash recorded a version for his 1974 album, accompanied by his wife, June Carter Cash, and his daughter, Roseanne Cash. June Carter Cash also recorded a version for her final solo album, *Wildwood Flower*. It was also featured in the movie *O Brother, Where Art Thou?*

Always keep on the sunny side.

YOU ARE MY SUNSHINE

You are my sunshine, my only sunshine

You make me happy when skies are gray

You'll never know Dear how much I love you

Please don't take my Sunshine away[4]

—Written in 1929 by Oliver Hood, a popular
musician from LaGrange, Georgia

OLIVER HOOD HAD EIGHT children and worked in a cotton
mill—not much money or sophistication. He never applied
for copyright and never received any compensation.[5]

Jimmie Davis, country music star and former governor
of Louisiana, filed and received rights to the song in 1939. It
is now the state song of Louisiana. Jimmy Davis's estate is still

---

4   Davis, Jimmie, and Charles Mitchell. "You Are My Sunshine."
Lyrics.com. Accessed August 28, 2022. https://www.lyrics.com/lyr-
ic/17927930/Bing+Crosby/You+Are+My+Sunshine.

5   "Songwriters and Music Legends of LaGrange." VisitLagrange.com.
Accessed September 8, 2022. https://www.visitlagrange.com/songwrit-
ers-and-music-legends-of-lagrange/.

receiving compensation every time "You Are My Sunshine" is recorded or used in a movie.

It has been recorded by Gene Autry, Bing Crosby, Lawrence Welk, Nat King Cole, Ray Charles, Andy Williams, Aretha Franklin, Anne Murray, Johnny Cash, Carly Simon, and many, many more.

In 1959, Oliver Hood wrote:

Somewhere the sun is shining.

But there's rain in my Heart today

There's no denying, my heart keeps crying

Somebody stole my Sunshine away

JOHNNY MERCER

JOHNNY MERCER WAS BORN in Savannah, Georgia, on November 18, 1909. He became very famous. There is a statue of Johnny Mercer located at Ellis Square in downtown Savannah. Johnny Mercer's niece and I worked at Belk-Lindsey department store in 1957. I sold boys' clothes, and she worked in the record department. She was a senior, and I was a sophomore. She was very pretty. However, I don't think she ever really knew my name.

Johnny Mercer wrote fifteen hundred songs. One of his many hits was "Moon River." My cousin lived on Moon River. Moon River is in Savannah. The song was featured in *Breakfast at Tiffany's*. His music is also in the movie *Midnight in the Garden of Good and Evil*, which was filmed in Savannah. He wrote the song "Days of Wine and Roses" for the movie *Days of Wine and Roses*; it won him four Oscars.

Just to list some of his songs you may recognize—"You Must Have Been a Beautiful Baby," "That Old Black Magic," "Come Rain or Come Shine," "Blues in the Night," "Rock-A-Bye Your Baby," "I'm in the Mood for Love," "Summer Wind," "Heartaches," "Autumn Leaves," "Ac-Cent-Tchu-Ate the Positive," "The Very Thought of You," "In The Cool, Cool, Cool of the Evening," "Jeepers Creepers," "Fools Rush in (Where Angels Fear to Tread)," "P.S. I Love You," and "Lazybones."

He wrote the lyrics for the Broadway play, *Seven Brides for Seven Brothers*, for which he won a Tony Award. He also wrote "One for My Baby (and One More for the Road)," recorded by Frank Sinatra. It was penned on a napkin while he was sitting at a bar lamenting a previous girlfriend. He wrote many, many others.

Johnny Mercer and Bing Crosby were very close friends. Johnny was Bing's favorite songwriter. Bing recorded over one hundred of Johnny's songs.

Barry Manilow's first hit, "Mandy," was written by Johnny and named after Johnny's daughter. Johnny also wrote the song "Charade" for the movie *Charade*, starring Audrey Hepburn and Cary Grant.

In 1942, Johnny founded Capital Records for $25,000. He sold it thirteen years later for $20 million. One of the first singers he signed at Capital Records was Nat King Cole.

Those were some of the good ole days.

THE LITTLE BROWN CHURCH

There's a church in the valley by the wildwood

No lovelier spot in the dale

No place is so dear to my childhood

As the Little Brown Church in the Vale

Oh, come to the Little Church in the Wildwood

Oh, come to the Little Brown Church in the Vale[6]

—Dr. William S. Pitts, *The Church in the Wildwood*, 1857

DR. PITTS WAS A medical student who sold the rights to the song for twenty-five dollars to help with his expenses. The Little Brown Church in the Vale is located in Nashua, Iowa.

Among those who found and loved the song at this time was the Weatherwax Quartet. They traveled all across Canada and the United States. They used "The Little Brown Church" as their trademark song. As the song became more and more popular, the Little Brown Church became a tourist and wed-

---

6   Pitts, William S. "The Church in the Wildwood." Public Domain.

ding destination. Since 1924, over seventy-two thousand weddings have been held there, and over seventy-five thousand tourists have visited the Little Brown Church.[7]

Every time I sing the song, it reminds me of my mother. We sang the song quite frequently in the small Methodist church where I grew up. I learned at a very early age that it was definitely in my best interest to attend church every Sunday with my mother; otherwise she knew how to make my life not much fun.

---

7   "History." Littlebrownchurch.org. Accessed August 28, 2022. https://littlebrownchurch.org/the-church/history/.

AMAZING GRACE

THE SONG "AMAZING GRACE" was written over 249 years ago, in 1772, by John Newton, a former slave trader. However, the last verse of the song "Amazing Grace" was not added until 1909. It was added by Mr. Edwin Excell. Mr. Edwin Excell was a music composer. However, Mr. Excell did not write the verse. Mr. Excell found the verse in a book written in 1852. The book was *Uncle Tom's Cabin*.

The book *Uncle Tom's Cabin* was given credit for starting the Civil War. It was written by Harriet Beecher Stowe. It is a story about a slave named Tom and his master named Simon Legree. Tom taught himself to read. He began to read the Bible and became a born-again Christian. He wanted to teach the other slaves to read. He wanted to teach the other slaves Christianity. Simon Legree did not want his slaves to learn to read. Simon Legree did not want his slaves to think for themselves. So he demanded Tom renounce his Christianity. Tom refused. Simon Legree had Tom beaten to death. While Tom was dying, he started singing the song "Amazing Grace." That's when Harriet Beecher Stowe added the last verse: "When we've been there ten thousand years, bright shining as the sun, we've no less days to sing God's praise, than when we first begun."

Harriet Beecher Stowe was raised in Cincinnati, Ohio. Cincinnati was the stopping-off place for the Underground

Railroad, which brought the runaway slaves out of the South into the North. Harriet's father was president of Lane Theological Seminary. Because of who her father was, she had the opportunity to meet the slaves and get to know the slaves. In 1851, Harriet's six-month-old daughter, Julie, died of colic. During her period of grief, she began to realize how hard it was for the slave women to have their babies taken away at such a young age. That inspired her to write the book *Uncle Tom's Cabin*.

The book *Uncle Tom's Cabin* spread like wildfire. It became a bestseller. People felt like they knew Tom; they despised Simon Legree. They became very passionate. They began to demand an end to slavery. A few years later, slavery was abolished.

After the Civil War and before Abraham Lincoln was assassinated, Harriet Beecher Stowe had the opportunity to meet Abraham Lincoln. Lincoln said to her, "So you're the little woman who wrote the book that started the war."[8] I'd like to think she replied to him, "I cannot take credit for it. It was written by God himself. I was merely his instrument."

Today, "Amazing Grace" is America's favorite song. It's sung roughly ten million times every year at different functions. It is one of the most recorded songs ever written. It has

---

8   The Ohio State University. "Harriett Beecher Stowe." ehistory.osu. edu. Accessed August 28, 2022. https://ehistory.osu.edu/articles/harriet-beecher-stowe-little-woman-who-wrote-book-started-great-war.

been recorded over sixty-five hundred times.[9] That might not mean much, but most songs are recorded once, some maybe ten times, maybe even one hundred times. However, very few songs are recorded sixty-five hundred times.

In December 1970, Judy Collins made a recording of the song "Amazing Grace." Less than a month later, in January 1971, it was on the top of the charts in America and England. After Judy Collins recorded "Amazing Grace," many others recorded it as well. Just to name a few: Elvis Presley, Dolly Parton, Johnny Cash, Rod Stewart, Mahalia Jackson, Aretha Franklin, Sam Cook. The list goes on and on and on.

The "Amazing Grace story" is certainly a heartwarming story. It's especially heartwarming to me. My mother's name was Mildred Louise Newton, and her family was from England. I often wonder if there is a family connection.

As Paul Harvey used to say, "Now you know the rest of the story."

---

9   Edwards, Joe. "What's the most recorded song ever? 'Amazing grace.'" Updated November 10, 2010.

FAB FIVE

ON MARCH 3, 2017, Adopt Kansas Kids put on their website five Kansas City siblings looking for an adoptive family: three brothers and two sisters, ages two to eleven. They were all in different foster homes and wanted to be adopted in one family together.

The Kansas City Star weekly newspaper featured an article, "Family Wanted." The article triggered a nationwide response that filled the voice mailbox with over fifteen hundred inquiries—more than the mailbox could hold. The article went viral and had over seven million hits as far away as Ireland and New Zealand. The kids became known as the "Fab Five."[10]

The State of Kansas Adoption Agency interviewed hundreds and hundreds of couples. Fourteen months later, on May 30, 2018, Toni and Jeff Whaley became the parents of "The Fab Five." Toni and Jeff were a childless couple who lived just outside Kansas City. Today the kids are doing great. Now they have each other, two loving parents, aunts, uncles, cousins, and two sets of grandparents. Toni and Jeff Whaley have never been happier.

---

10   Associated Press. "Local Kansas Couple Adopts 'Fab Five' Siblings After Newspaper Story Spurs Worldwide Interest." Updated May 31, 2018. https://news.yahoo.com/local-kansas-couple-adopts-apos-000241401.html.

A few famous people who were adopted you may recognize: Babe Ruth, world's most famous baseball player; Steve Jobs, founder of Apple; Eleanor Roosevelt, longest-serving First Lady of the United States; Nelson Mandela, president of South Africa from 1994–1999; Michael Oher, former NFL player and subject of the movie *The Blind Side*; John Hancock, signer of the Declaration of Independence; Dave Thomas, founder of Wendy's; Edgar Allan Poe, American writer known for poetry and short stories.

Famous adoptive parents: Barbara Walters; Dolores and Bob Hope; Burt Reynolds and Loni Anderson; Diane Keaton; Angelina Jolie and Brad Pitt.

Jane and I are adoptive parents. We have one boy and one girl. We adopted each when they were three months old—three years apart. They both graduated from college and are married. Today we have three wonderful grandchildren. We are truly blessed.

THE GOOD OLD DAYS

FROM TIME TO TIME, we hear people say they want Highlands the way it used to be during the good old days. I can certainly understand. There are many of us who remember our towns and cities back in the forties, fifties, and early sixties. We can talk to our friends from Atlanta, Savannah (my hometown), Jacksonville, Orlando, Memphis, and on and on and on. These places are no longer the same.

I spent every summer back in the middle forties and early fifties with my grandparents in Swainsboro, Georgia. Swainsboro had a beautiful courthouse and very nice mom-and-pop stores on the square. It was easy to find just about anything that was needed. There were also two wonderful pharmacies with soda fountains. We went almost every day for milkshakes. Today, all of it is gone, including the courthouse. The mom-and-pop stores have been replaced with a large Walmart on the edge of town.

The American soda fountains started way back around 1850. At one time, there were thousands and thousands of locally owned pharmacies with soda fountains.[11] Stop in ev-

---

11   Soderlund Drugstore Museum. "History of the Soda Fountain." Accessed August 20, 2022. http://www.drugstoremuseum.com/soda-fountain/.

ery day after school, have a milkshake or sundae with your friends—special, special days. The soda fountains in America had completely collapsed by 1970.[12]

I have very fond memories of the five-and-ten-cent stores. F. W. Woolworth opened their first successful store in 1879 in Lancaster, Pennsylvania. They grew to over eight hundred stores. They went out of business in 1997. S. H. Kress five-and-ten-cent stores opened their first store in 1896 in Nanticoke, Pennsylvania. They grew to 264 stores. They went out of business in 1981.[13]

I also miss Morrison's Cafeterias. Their first store opened in 1920 in Mobile, Alabama. At one time, they had 151 locations in thirteen states. They finally went out of business in 1996 after a long, hard struggle to survive.[14]

Let's not forget Sears and the Sears catalog. There was a Sears store in Highlands owned by Mr. and Mrs. Alan Lewis. They had four children. Some of you may remember them—

---

12   O'Neil, Darcy. "Soda Fountain History." Updated December 14, 2010. https://www.artofdrink.com/soda/chapter-1-introduction.

13   Britannica. "Woolworth Co." Encyclopedia Britannica. Updated May 26, 2014. https://www.britannica.com/topic/Woolworth-Co.

14   "Morrison's Cafeteria-1945." Encyclopedia of Alabama. Accessed August 20, 2022. http://www.encyclopediaofalabama.org/article/m951#:~:text=Morrison%27s%20Cafeteria%20was%20founded%20by%20J.%20A.%20Morrison,company%20and%20the%20discontinuation%20of%20the%20Morrison%27s%20name.

Martha, Angie, Bill, and Scott. Angie is in the process of writing a book on growing up in Highlands in the good old days. How about Montgomery Ward? Today we have Amazon. Wow! Who would ever have believed? Don't forget pay phones.

Change is inevitable. Most places we remember have not changed for the better. However, I feel Highlands has been moving forward in a very positive way. In many ways, we are still like a town of yesteryear. Many kids can walk to school. Parents are still involved. Most people in town all know each other. The Rotary Clubs and other charitable organizations are very involved and supportive. We are in a bubble. It is a blessing indeed to live in Highlands, North Carolina.

SUMMERVILLE, SOUTH CAROLINA—THE BIRTHPLACE OF SWEET TEA

IN THE HEART OF the low country, there is a place where flowers bloom by the acre, and history lives on every corner, where world-class cuisine is served with a side of southern charm and sweet tea is measured by the gallon. The name of the place is Summerville, South Carolina.

Summerville is the birthplace of sweet tea. Every year there is a Sweet Tea Festival. Over fifteen thousand people show up to celebrate sweet tea. Summerville is also the home of Mason, the largest known container of sweet tea. Mason stands over fifteen feet tall and can hold up to 2,524 gallons of sweet tea.[15] Dolly Parton calls sweet tea the champagne of the South.

Mason is located on the Sweet Tea Trail. On the trail, businesses serve sweet tea specials, including sweet tea cupcakes, sweet tea cinnamon rolls, sweet tea jelly, a sweet tea porkchop sandwich, and even a sweet tea-brined chicken salad. While on the Sweet Tea Trail, visitors like to pose for a photo with Mason.

---

15   VisitSummerville.com, Accessed August 20, 2022. www.visitsummerville.com/sweet-tea-trail.

The first place in the United States to achieve long-term tea production was in Summerville, at Dr. Charles Shepard's Pinehurst Tea Plantation.[16] Dr. Shepard was a respected botanist, chemist, lecturer, and writer. His love of horticulture and his meticulous nature influenced every farm-related function for processing tea. South Carolina is the only state that commercially produces tea on a mass-market scale. Summerville is now in the Guinness World Records book for serving more sweet tea in one day than any other place in the world.[17]

Just to prove that Americans take their tea seriously, you must remember the Boston Tea Party. On December 16, 1773, at Griffin's Wharf, American colonists dumped 342 chests of tea imported by the British East India Company into the harbor. They were showing Great Britain that Americans wouldn't take taxation and tyranny without a fight.

How about the favorite drink at the Kentucky Derby? The mint julep is a mixture of crushed ice, lemon slices, mint sprigs, bourbon, and of course, sweet tea.

The low country is also the birthplace of Hoppin' John, Charleston light dragoon punch, she-crab soup, chicken bog, benne wafers, Frogmore Stew, and, yes, even shrimp and grits.

I always liked the song "Tea for Two," by Vincent Youmans. It was one of the more popular songs for decades. It was

---

16   L, Mary. "History of Tea in the USA." TopicTea. Accessed August 20, 2022.http://topictea.com/blogs/tea-blog/history-of-tea-in-the-usa./

17   VisitSummerville.com, Accessed August 20, 2022. https://www.visitsummerville.com/sweet-tea-trail.

written in 1924 and later made into a movie starring Doris Day.

GIRL SCOUTS OF AMERICA

GIRL SCOUTS IN THE United States of America began on March 12, 1912, when Juliette "Daisy" Gordon Low organized the first Girl Guide meeting of eighteen girls in Savannah, Georgia. Juliette Gordon Low envisioned an organization that would prepare girls to meet the world with courage, confidence, and character. At the time, women in the United States could not even vote. Women were expected to be housewives and mothers or, until they got married, to be teachers, nurses, or secretaries. Actually, at one time, once married, they could no longer teach school. What were the men thinking?

The girls played basketball. They hiked, swam, and camped. They learned to read the world around them—for instance, by studying a foreign language and telling time by the stars. Research shows the inclusive, all-female environment of a Girl Scout troop creates a safe space where girls can try new things, develop a range of skills, take on leadership positions, and even feel allowed to fail, dust themselves off, get up, and try again. In other words, Girl Scouts work. It's the best leadership experience for girls in the world for one very good reason: because it's girl led!

During World War II, many young Japanese American girls were confined in internment camps with their families.

Girl Scout troops were even organized in these camps. Thousands of young Japanese girls became Girl Scouts.

Today the small gathering of girls that Juliette Gordon Low hosted over a century ago has grown into a global movement that today includes 2.6 million Girl Scouts in ninety-two countries and more than fifty million alums,[18] united across distance and decades by lifelong friendships, shared adventures, and the desire to do big things to make the world a better place.

One of the many Girl Scout projects is selling Girl Scout cookies. In 2020, Girl Scouts sold over two hundred million boxes of cookies. The net profit to Girl Scouts was $600 million. Girls learn from selling cookies—goal setting, decision making, money management, people skills, and business ethics.[19]

Katie Francis holds the career record for the number of Girl Scout cookies sold with a total of 180,000 boxes. In 2014, she broke the single season record by selling 21,477 boxes, then broke that record the next year selling 22,200 boxes.[20]

18   Girl Scouts of America. "Facts about Girl Scouts." Girl Scouts of America. Accessed August 20, 2022. https://www.girlscouts.org/en/footer/faq/facts.html.

19   Schmidt, Ann. "Girl Scout Cookies and what to know about the $800 million business." Fox Business. Updated March 12, 2020. https://www.foxbusiness.com/lifestyle/girl-scout-cookies-what-to-know.

20   Francis, Katie. "About Katie." Katie Francis (blog). Accessed August 20, 2022.
https://katiefrancis.com/about-katie/.

She sold the record-breaking box to Jimmy Fallon while being interviewed on the *Tonight Show*.

The initial incentive that inspired Katie in 2011 was a college scholarship. However, she soon learned that her commitment to selling cookies was helping her accomplish her dream of supporting her Girl Scout Council's efforts in building a new urban camp. She is always trying to learn as much as she can and has participated in the Sandler Training Foundations Course, a course designed to improve sales performance.

In addition to selling Girl Scout cookies, Katie is an excellent student and maintained straight As in high school. She loves to perform and studies piano, flute, and voice. She took thirteen years of dance classes, including jazz, tap, ballet, and Irish dance.

While being interviewed on a local radio show, Katie was asked what her secret was. How did she sell so many boxes of Girl Scout cookies? She replied, "I just asked."

"No, really Katie, how do you do it?"

Katie said, "I asked everybody."

Another heartwarming story is about Daisy Emery. Daisy Emery is deaf. Daisy had to transfer from the deaf school she had been attending since she was six months old to a new public school. As you may imagine, it was not easy. Every day, Daisy would come home from school angry, upset, and often in tears. She was not fitting in. However, on Girl Scout meeting days, her life began to change. Her mom said the Girl Scouts made her feel accepted, loved, and important. They helped

Emery feel she was special. Emery's mom said the Girl Scouts gave Emery a new life. I'm sure it also gave Emery's mother a new life.

When Eva St. Clair was nine years old, she spent her birthday money (fifty dollars) at Goodwill on a 1948 sewing machine. She didn't even know how to sew. The Girl Scouts taught her. Sewing became her passion. After graduating from Stanford University, Eva decided she wanted to become a costume designer. Today, Eva is CEO of Princess Awesome, a worldwide company that designs and sells girls' clothes. Eva said she can't wait to become a troop leader when her daughter is old enough to join Girl Scouts. (The success stories go on and on.)

Fifty-two percent of female business leaders were Girl Scouts; 60 percent of US senators and 100 percent of Secretaries of State were Girl Scouts.[21]

Just to name a few famous Girl Scouts: Queen Elizabeth II, Sally Ride (first American woman in space), Debbie Reynolds, Mary Tyler Moore, Ann Landers, Martha Stewart, Lucille Ball, Grace Kelly, Barbara Walters, Jane Pauley, Laura Bush, Condoleezza Rice, Nancy Reagan, Janet Reno (America's first female attorney general), Sandra Day O'Connor (first female Supreme Court justice), Katie Couric, Dionne Warwick, Carrie Fisher, Madeline Albright, Bette Davis, Lynda Carter

---

21 Girl Scouts of America. Accessed August 20, 2022. https://www.girlscouts.org.

(Wonder Woman), Gwyneth Paltrow, and the list goes on and on and on.

There are many more stories I could share. However, this gives you an idea of the importance of Girl Scouts, not only in America but in the whole world. Thank God for the Girl Scouts.

THE CHURCH THAT WAS MOVED BY THE HAND OF GOD

SWAN QUARTER, NORTH CAROLINA, is a very small farming and fishing community located on Pamlico Sound. Pamlico Sound eventually goes out to the Atlantic Ocean to Nags Head and Cape Hatteras, which is on the Outer Banks of North Carolina. Swan Quarter is known as being in the Inner Banks of North Carolina.

Swan Quarter is the county seat for Hyde County. Hyde County may be the largest county in North Carolina but may have the smallest population. There are only about five thousand people in Hyde County. There isn't one traffic light in the entire county. However, Hyde County also has the largest natural lake in North Carolina—Lake Mattamuskeet. Lake Mattamuskeet is in a wildlife preserve. At certain times of the year there are so many ducks, geese, and wild swans on the lake that one can hardly see the water—hence the name Swan Quarter.

Swan Quarter has survived two major hurricanes. The last one was Hurricane Isabel in 2003. Many homes were completely destroyed and many businesses severely damaged. Swan Quarter has also survived a number of floods. Because of the floods, many homes are built on stilts. Also, today, because of the floods, there is a dike separating Swan Quarter from Pamlico Sound.

Swan Quarter was settled in the early 1700s. In 1874, a group of Methodists decided they wanted to build a new church in downtown Swan Quarter. The property they wanted to buy had a beautiful view overlooking Pamlico Sound. However, the property was owned by Mr. Sam Sadler, and Mr. Sadler did not want to sell his property. The more the church tried to buy Mr. Sadler's property, the more determined Mr. Sadler was not to sell.

Finally, the church bought another property located about three blocks from Mr. Sadler. They built their new church. On September 16, 1876, they had a dedication of the new church and named the church the Methodist Episcopal Church of Swan Quarter, North Carolina.

Three days later, there was a flood. The floodwaters picked up the church, and it started to float right down the main street of Swan Quarter. Ms. Leila Bren, who was born and raised in Swan Quarter, was standing in her kitchen looking out her kitchen window. She saw the church floating right past her house. She watched it take a left, go about a block, and sit right down on the property owned by Mr. Sam Sadler. Many say that Mr. Sadler was so in awe that he gave the property to the church. They changed the name of the church from the Methodist Episcopal Church of Swan Quarter to the Providence Methodist Church of Swan Quarter.

I had the opportunity to visit the Providence Methodist Church of Swan Quarter. It is still one of the most active churches in Swan Quarter today. When you walk in the entrance of the church, right above the door is a plaque that reads "The Church That Was Moved by the Hand of God."

LIFE

I REMEMBER I COULD hardly wait until I reached sixteen and could get my driver's license. I was so excited to graduate from high school. Wow, would I ever finish college? Some people suffer exquisite trauma when they reach the big four-oh or that fearful fifty. When does life really begin? Life begins the first time and every time we find a reason for living—a goal, a purpose, a mission, a desire that excites, a desire that energizes, a desire that gives us courage.

All happy events create a new life, one that might last for decades or might end in a few memorable moments. Each of them either has passed or will pass in time. The same is true of unpleasant events. They may be long or short in duration. They are all destined to pass away.

So we don't—or shouldn't—live just one life. We have the opportunity to live hundreds of lives or thousands of them during our visit to this small planet. After all, Grandma Moses started to paint when she was well past retirement age. People become clergy at seventy. Some enter college in their sixties, and some run their first marathons after that big four-oh. Such people always look ahead to the lives they will spend rather than back at the lives that have been spent.

I like the sad epitaph about a man who didn't share this point of view:

How sad that he died at forty,

With most of his living undone.

But sadder still that he hung around...

To be buried at eighty-one

'TWAS THE NIGHT
BEFORE CHRISTMAS

'Twas the night before Christmas, when all thro' the house,

Not a creature was stirring, not even a mouse;

The stockings were hung by the chimney with care,

In hopes that St. Nicholas soon would be there;

The children were nestled all snug in their beds,

While visions of sugar plums danc'd in their heads,

And mama in her 'kerchief, and I in my cap,

Had just settled down for a long winter nap—

When out on the lawn there arose such a clatter,

I sprang from the bed to see what was the matter.

Away to the window I flew like a flash,

Tore open the shutters, and threw up the sash.

The moon on the breast of the new fallen snow,

Gave the lustre of mid-day to objects below;

When, what to my wondering eyes should appear,

But a miniature sleigh, and eight tiny reindeer,

With a little old driver, so lively and quick,

I knew in a moment it must be St. Nick.

More rapid than eagles his coursers they came:

And he whistled, and shouted, and call'd them by name:

"Now Dasher, now Dancer, now Prancer, and Vixen,

On Comet, on Cupid, on Donner and Blitzen;

To the top of the porch, to the top of the wall,

Now dash away! dash away! dash away all."

So up to the house-top the coursers they flew,

With the sleigh full of toys—and St. Nicholas too,

And then in a twinkling, I heard on the roof

The prancing and pawing of each little hoof.

As I drew my head, and was turning around,

Down the chimney St. Nicholas came with a bound:

He was dress'd all in fur, from his head to his foot,

And his clothes were all tarnish'd with ashes and soot;

A bundle of toys was flung on his back,

And he looked like a peddler just opening his pack:

His eyes—how they twinkled! His dimples how merry,

His cheeks were like roses, his nose like a cherry;

His droll little mouth was drawn up like a bow,

And the beard of his chin was white as the snow;

He had a broad face, and a little round belly

That shook when he laugh'd, like a bowl full of jelly:

A wink of his eyes and a twist of his head

Soon gave me to know I had nothing to dread.

He spoke not a word, but went straight to his work,

And fill'd all the stockings; then turn'd with a jerk.

And laying his finger aside his nose

And giving a nod, up the chimney he rose.

He sprung to his sleigh, to his team gave a whistle,

And away they all flew, like the down of a thistle:

But I heard him exclaim, ere he drove out of sight—

Happy Christmas to all, and to all a good night.[22]

---

22 Moore, Clement Clark. The Night Before Christmas. New York City: G.P. Putnam's Sons, 1998.

***

WE CELEBRATE CHRISTMAS TO honor the birth of the baby Jesus. The first recorded date of Christmas being celebrated on December 25 was in Rome, AD 336. Constantine was emperor of Rome (he was the first Christian Roman Emperor). Germany is credited with starting the Christmas tree as we know it today sometime in the 1500s.

One of the most popular Christmas movies is *Miracle on 34th Street*. It was released in 1947. It won three Academy Awards.

It stars Maureen O'Hara, John Payne, and Natalie Wood. Natalie Wood was just eight years old.

EARL OF SANDWICH

IT'S HARD TO BELIEVE that we Americans eat over three hundred million sandwiches every day. That's right: every day we consume about as many sandwiches as we have people to eat them. And why not? The sandwich may be the perfect food. There is a sandwich for every occasion. It's popular at parties, picnics, church socials, schoolkids' lunches, and many, many other events.

The sandwich has a long history. The sandwich as we know it was popularized in England in 1762 by John Montagu. John Montagu was the fourth Earl of Sandwich. Earl of Sandwich is a noble title in the peerage of England.

In 1762, John Montagu invented the meal that changed dining forever. John Montagu was a gambler. He could play cards all night and never leave the table. He ordered his valet to bring him meat tucked between two pieces of bread. Lord Sandwich was fond of this form of food because it allowed him to continue playing his cards while eating without a fork and only using one hand. This form of food became so popular that soon people would just say, "Bring me a sandwich."

The sandwich's popularity in Spain and England increased dramatically during the nineteenth century, when the rise of industrial society and the working classes made fast, portable, and inexpensive meals essential. In London, by 1850, at least seventy vendors were selling sandwiches on the streets. Also at that time, sandwiches were becoming popular in Holland and America.

John Montagu XI is the Earl of Sandwich today. He serves in the House of Lords. John Montagu is still considered an English aristocrat. He and his youngest son, Orlando, have started franchising Earl of Sandwich restaurants. The first Earl of Sandwich opened on March 19, 2004, in downtown Disney. Today there are thirty-seven existing locations.

When I worked for the railroad, I took a bag of sandwiches to work every day. All railroad men did. We also would have a big thermos of coffee.

What are you going to have for lunch today? I think I will have a sandwich—maybe two.

JINGLE BELLS

"JINGLE BELLS" WAS WRITTEN by James Lord Pierpont in 1857. The original name was "One Horse Open Sleigh." It was written to be sung by a Sunday School choir or maybe even to be sung as a drinking song.

However, it became associated with Christmas music in the 1860s and 1870s. It soon became the most popular and recognized Christmas song to ever be written, not only in the United States but around the world. In recognition for his achievement, James Lord Pierpont was voted into the Songwriters Hall of Fame.

"Jingle Bells" was first recorded in 1889 by Will Lyle. The song soon became a Christmas favorite. In 1935, Benny Goodman and His Orchestra reached number eighteen on the top 100 music charts. In 1941, Glen Miller and the Modernaires reached number five on the top 100 music charts. In 1943, Bing Crosby and the Andrews Sisters sold over one million copies. In 2006, Kimberley Locke's recording reached number one, and many voted it the "Song of the Year."

It was the first song broadcast from space. The astronauts on *Gemini VI*, while in space on December 16, 1965, sent a report to mission control: "This is Gemini VI. We have an object—looks like a satellite going from north to south, up a polar orbit. Is it a sleigh? I think we hear music." The astronauts then produced a smuggled harmonica and sleigh bells and broadcast a rendition of "Jingle Bells."

Dashing thro' the snow

In a one-horse open sleigh,

Over the fields we go,

Laughing all the way;

Bells on bobtail ring,

making spirits bright,

Oh, what fun it is to ride and sing

A sleighing song tonight.

Jingle bells, jingle bells,

Jingle all the way;

Oh what fun it is to ride

In a one-horse open sleigh

DAYLIGHT SAVING TIME

YIPES! IT'S THAT TIME of year again. On the first Sunday of November, we have to adjust our clocks. Do we move up an hour or back an hour? I can never remember. And is it only twice a year? It seems like more.

The very first time of daylight saving was mentioned by Benjamin Franklin in the spring of 1784. He was visiting Paris, France, and mentioned "time change" in an essay he wrote. He suggested Parisians change their sleep schedule to save money on candles and lamp oil.

The first city in the world to adopt daylight saving time was Port Arthur, Ontario, Canada, on July 1, 1908. Soon other cities in Canada adopted daylight saving time. Germany adopted daylight saving time on April 30, 1916, to conserve coal during World War I. The United States adopted daylight saving time in 1918 during World War I. However, Arizona and Hawaii refused to honor daylight saving time, and they still don't today.

The proponents of daylight saving time argue that longer evenings motivate people to get out and get involved. The extra hour of daylight can be used for outdoor recreation like golf, soccer, baseball, and other activities. The tourism industry profits from longer evenings. The retail industry benefits because people have a tendency to shop more.

The facts are, though, that lack of sleep causes more auto accidents, more workplace injuries, suicides, heart attacks, strokes, and miscarriages, among other health problems. Maybe it has something to do with stress. I know I get a little stressed trying to decide to adjust clocks forward or backward.

Many states have passed state laws to have only standard time or only daylight saving time during the year. Some states want year-round standard time, and some want year-round daylight saving time. The states are waiting for federal approval. I say, "What's the big deal?" Let each state do what they want. Today when it is 9:00 p.m. in Highlands, North Carolina, it is 6:00 p.m. in California. That seems to work OK.

Peggy Boquist, wife and legislative assistant for state senator Brian Boquist, who supports a bill to lock in daylight saving year round, said, "Changing the time on our clocks twice a year does only one good thing, in my humble opinion: it reminds me to change the batteries in my smoke alarms."[23]

Personally, I don't really care. Just don't make me change all my clocks twice a year.

---

23   Wei-Haas, Maya. "Tired of Daylight Saving Time? These Places Are Trying to End It." Science. National Geographic, May 3, 2021. https://www.nationalgeographic.com/science/article/tired-of-daylight-saving-time-these-states-trying-to-end-clock-changes.

THE KINGS INN

I'M SURE ALL OF you who have lived in Highlands before 1994 remember the Kings Inn. It was located at Fourth and South Streets. It burned down in 1994. It was originally built by Mr. Monroe Skinner as his home. Mr. Skinner moved to Highlands from Wyoming in 1878. He became the justice of the peace and tax collector for Highlands.

Mrs. Margaretta Ravenel bought Mr. Skinner's home in 1883 and christened it "the Islington House." She named it after an old section of Charleston, South Carolina. She turned it into one of Highlands's most gracious lodgings. Mr. R. R. "Bob" King bought it in 1925. Mr. King made it into a very luxurious hotel and named it the Kings Inn. It became the number one hotel in Highlands. It was the first hotel to have a heated swimming pool. It also had a television and fireplace in each room.

The Kings Inn became the honeymoon capital of western North Carolina. In the forties and fifties, anywhere from twenty-five to forty newlyweds would celebrate their honeymoons at the Kings Inn every year. Mrs. King became known for her southern cooking. The dining room seated 150 people. On Sundays, people would come from miles away to enjoy Mrs. King's Sunday buffet. Her recipes are still floating around

Highlands, and you can order her cookbook online (*King's Inn Cookbook*).

In 1940, Mr. and Mrs. Robert E. Edwards were celebrating their sixtieth wedding anniversary at the Kings Inn. Almost everyone in Highlands was invited. At that time the population was a little over five hundred. During the celebration, a young man walked up to Mr. Edwards and said, "Mr. Edwards, you are truly a hero. You have the perfect marriage. What is your secret?"

Mr. Edwards looked at him and said, "Son, it is really simple. In 1880 we got married at the log law house. [The log law house was built in 1850 and served as a schoolhouse, courthouse, church, and community center. There were no churches in Highlands in 1880 and very few places to have wedding ceremonies. The log law house was located where Wright's Square is located today.] When we left to go on our honeymoon, we had a brand-new buggy and a brand-new mule. We got about a hundred yards out of town, and the mule stopped; it wouldn't budge. My wife jumped out of the buggy, got in front of the mule, looked him in the eye and said, 'That's one.'

"The mule went about another fifty yards and stopped again. My wife jumped out of the buggy, got in the mule's face, looked him the eye, and said, 'That's two.' The third time, the mule went about fifty yards and stopped again. My wife jumped out of the buggy, got in the mule's face, took a pistol out of her purse, and shot the mule three times. I jumped out of the buggy and said, 'Sweetheart, you can't do that.' My wife looked at me and said, 'That's one.'

"You are right. We have had a perfect marriage for sixty years."

WE NEED HEROES

THE TERM HERO COMES from the ancient Greeks. For them, a hero was a mortal who had done something so far beyond the normal scope of human experience that he left an immortal memory behind after he died and thus received worship like that due the gods. Heroes were always extraordinary. To be a hero was to expand people's sense of what was possible for a human being.

Hercules may be the first known hero of all heroes. The Romans built statues of Hercules as early as 305 BC. Hercules was the champion of the weak. He was famous for his strength. He was much like Samson, except Hercules had no weaknesses. He always stood for what was right. Marvel Comics published a Hercules comic book in 1958. In 1995 there was a Hercules TV program, and Disney made a movie of Hercules in 1997.

I grew up in the early 1940s and 1950s. I had plenty of heroes. My first heroes were my parents and grandparents. But I also had Roy Rogers, Dale Evans (and Trigger), Gene Autry, Batman and Robin, Superman, Spiderman, and I must include Wonder Woman. The good always won in the end.

The TV shows were family shows. At night my family and I watched the shows together. In those days, TV shows gave examples of how we were supposed to live. The shows I remember watching were shows like *Leave It to Beaver*, *The*

Howdy Doody Show, The Adventures of Ozzie and Harriet, Father Knows Best, Lassie, The Ed Sullivan Show, and others.

Heroes give us examples of how we are supposed to live and to act; they inspire us, motivate us, and encourage us to transform ourselves for the better and put the welfare of others before ourselves.

Mother Teresa was certainly a hero. This excerpt is taken from the Nobel Prize website: She was born in Skopje, Macedonia, on August 26, 1910. At the age of twelve, she felt strongly the call of God. She knew she had to be a missionary to spread the love of Christ. At the age of eighteen, she left her parents and joined the Sisters of Loreto, a community of nuns and missions in India. After a few months of training in Dublin, she was sent to Calcutta. There, she started working among the poorest of the poor in the slums of Calcutta. In 1950 she received permission from the Vatican to start her own order, "the Missions of Charity," whose task was to love and care for those persons no one was prepared to look after. In 1965 the society became an International Religious Family by a decree of Pope Paul VI.

The Society of Missionaries has spread all over the world, including the former Soviet Union and countries in Asia, Africa, and Latin America. They take care of the shut-ins, alcoholics, homeless, and AIDS sufferers.

The Missionaries of Charity throughout the world are aided and assisted by the International Association of Co-Workers of Mother Teresa, which became an official international association on March 29, 1969. By the 1990s there were over one million Co-Workers in more than forty countries.

Mother Teresa's work has been recognized and acclaimed throughout the world. She has received a number of awards. In 2016, Mother Teresa was declared a saint by Pope Francis.[24]

Mother Teresa dedicated her entire life to helping the poor and down and out. She truly is a saint.

A hero is somebody who is selfless, who is generous in spirit, who tries to give back as much as possible, and someone who really cares. A hero can be an ordinary individual who finds the strength to persevere and endure in spite of overwhelming obstacles.

It doesn't take a hero to order men in battle. It takes a hero to be one of those men who goes into battle.

—Norman Schwarzkopf

---

24   Nobel Lectures, Peace 1971-1980, Editor-in-Charge Tore Fräng-smyr, Editor Irwin Abrams, World Scientific Publishing Co., Singapore, 1997

MOTHER'S DAY

MOTHER'S DAY WAS STARTED by Anna Jarvis in 1908 to honor her mother.[25] She actually started the concept of Mother's Day in the 1800s by hosting a "Mother's Day Work Club" to teach young mothers how to take care of their children. She was a peace activist who cared for wounded soldiers on both sides of the Civil War. Anna wanted to keep the tradition going. In 1914, President Wilson signed a proclamation designating Mother's Day, celebrated on the second Sunday in May, as a national holiday.[25]

Yes, we all go home to Mother

When the day is near it's close

For 'tis there we get our comfort

And a balm for all our woes.

How we need her to be with us!

For her counsel we would fly,

For we feel the need of mother

25   History. "Mother's Day." History.com. Updated April 29, 2011. https://www.history.com/topics/holidays/mothers-day.

Every day that passes by.

There's none else can so determine

What all our needs is best.

None so truly sympathizes

When we are facing some great test.

In our days of early childhood

We felt no need of other,

But brought our troubles and our joys

And emptied them on Mother.

She it was who kissed our bruises,

Binding up each cut and sprain;

Gladly she'd have borne our suffering,

Freeing us from ache and pain.

Her smiles would chase away our tears,

With her the sun was shining;

It mattered not if clouds were black,

MOTHER'S DAY

She saw the silver lining.

And always so very gentle,

With her hand upon our brow;

She would speak the words of wisdom

Just like the benedictions now

Oh, how she loved us everyone,

We can never quite forget

Such love as hers can know no end

But, lingers with us yet

The years have come, the years have gone

And Mother is now sleeping,

Her place is vacant in our home

Sad vigil we are keeping

The bit of comfort we do find,

We'd swap it for no other,

We'll pledge ourselves to live like her

And then—go home to Mother

—Ossie McCord McLarty, the grandmother
of my wife, Jane, 1942

THANKSGIVING

THANKSGIVING HAS TO BE one of everyone's favorites—no pressure to buy that special gift, just get together with family and friends and count our many, many blessings.

Thanksgiving was declared a national holiday by President Abraham Lincoln in 1863 during the American Civil War. He proclaimed it to be a day of "Thanksgiving and Praise to our beneficent Father who dwelled in the Heavens." The first Thanksgiving was celebrated by the Pilgrims after their first harvest in the New World in 1621. It was attended by ninety Native Americans and fifty-three Pilgrims. It was a day of prayer and thanking God.[26,27]

26   Krull, Kyle. "Wishing You and Yours a Blessed Thanksgiving." KyleKrull.com. Updated November 25, 2021. https://www.kylekrull. com/wishing-you-and-yours-a-blessed-thanksgiving/#:~:text=In%20 the%20midst%20of%20the%20conflict%20known%20as,all%20Americans%20on%20the%20last%20Thursday%20of%20November.

27   Wikipedia. "Thanksgiving" Wikipedia.org. Accessed August 25, 2022.
https://en.wikipedia.org/wiki/Thanksgiving#In_the_United_States.

When I started counting my blessings,
my whole life turned around.

—Willie Nelson

Be thankful for what you have, you'll end up
having more. If you concentrate on what you
don't have, you will never have enough.

—Oprah Winfrey

The greatest source of happiness is the
ability to be grateful at all times.

—Zig Ziglar

In everything give thanks; for this is the will
of God in Christ Jesus concerning you.

—1 Thessalonians 5:18(KJV)

I like the taste of turkey

Anytime throughout the year

But it never seems to taste as good

As when Thanksgiving is here.

Could it be it's cooked with all the trimmings

That are cooked with it to eat—

But I think it's eating at Grandma's house

That makes it such a treat[28]

WISHING EVERYONE A HAPPY Thanksgiving. May all of you have many rich blessings, peace, and prosperity throughout all the days of your lives.

28 "At Grandma's House." Loving2Learn.com. Accessed October 13, 2022. http://www.loving2learn.com/Activities/Thanksgiving/ThanksgivingPoems/AtGrandmasHouse.aspx

REMEMBERING ANN LANDERS

I MISS ANN LANDERS. The woman who popularized the column was actually the second to write under that pseudonym. Her real name was Esther "Eppie" Friedman. She was born on July 4, 1918, in Sioux City, Iowa. She had a twin sister who later became Abby in Dear Abby. In 1955, when she was thirty-seven years old, Esther entered a contest put on by the *Chicago Sun Times* to see who would take the place of the original "Ann Landers," who had recently passed away. Of course, Esther won the contest. About two years after she became the new Ann Landers, her sister started a Dear Abby column. This really upset Esther; she didn't think it was right for her sister to go in competition with her. However, they soon got that resolved, and like most twins, they were very, very close.

Dear Abby, though, never reached the popularity and status of Ann Landers. Esther, as Ann Landers, became the number one columnist in the world. She wrote six best-selling books. My favorite was *Wake Up and Smell the Coffee*. She was on two presidential councils—Presidents Nixon and Carter. *Psychology Today* said she helped more people solve their problems than anyone ever had, and *The World Almanac* said she was the most influential woman in America. Before she died, she was receiving over two thousand letters every day.

I just want to share with you one of those letters.

Dear Ann Landers, I am a boy 12 years of age. I recently did something my parents did not think was right, and the punishment was they made me stay home from a ball game I was dying to see. The tickets were already bought so they took my cousin instead of me. It was the worst day of my life. I thought they were terrible to treat me so bad. So, I decided to pack my suitcase and run away. I finished packing and thought maybe I ought to write a goodbye note. I wanted my parents to know why I was running away. As I was writing, I thought about all kinds of things. I then thought to be fair, I should thank them for the nice things they had done for me. It seemed like more than I could count. I then thought I should apologize for a few things I had done that was not right. It seemed like an awful lot of them.

I finished writing, unpacked my suitcase then tore up what I wrote. I hope all kids that think they want to run away from home will sit down and write their parents a note like I did, then maybe they won't go.

Signed "A Rotten Kid"[29]

---

29   Landers, Ann. "Signed the Rotten Kid." The Best of Ann Landers: Her Favorite Letters of All Time. New York, NY: Fawcett Columbine, 1997.

ANN LANDERS WROTE BACK: "Dear Kid, you don't sound so rotten to me; as a matter of fact, you sound like the kind of kid I would love to have as my own."

A few of Ann Landers favorite quotes:

"My personal recipe for success is do what you love and don't look at the clock"

"When life's problems seem overwhelming, look around you and see what other people are coping with."

"Opportunities are usually disguised as hard work, so many people do not recognize them."

PHYLLIS DILLER

PHYLLIS DRIVER, BETTER KNOWN to us as Phyllis Diller, passed away a few years ago at age ninety-five. She was a very gifted comedian and a gifted entertainer. She was also a wonderful mother. She had five children, and they all loved her dearly. She got her start as a guest on the Groucho Marx TV show. That show launched her career. She was in forty-two movies, entertained on Broadway (leading lady in *Hello, Dolly!*), had two different TV programs, and was a guest over one hundred times on different TV shows.[30] She was one of Johnny Carson's favorites as well as of Bob Hope and Ed Sullivan. At one time she had her own radio program. She was a concert pianist. She appeared as a piano soloist with symphony orchestras across the country between 1971 and1981. The *San Francisco Examiner* called her a fine concert pianist with a firm touch. She wrote five best-selling books as well as stories for *Ellery Queen's Mystery Magazine* (I remember reading all *Ellery Queen's* mysteries). She was a gifted artist. She toured with Bob Hope entertaining the US troops overseas. Phyllis Diller was a true, loyal American and role model.

---

30   Wikipedia. "Phyllis Diller." Wikipedia.org. Accessed August 25, 2022.
https://en.wikipedia.org/wiki/Phyllis_Diller.

She credits the book *The Magic of Thinking Big*, by Claude M. Bristol, for giving her the confidence she needed to move forward as a stand-up comedian. She is quoted as saying, "I know *The Magic of Thinking Big* made a positive difference in my life." She was the first female stand-up comedian. Joan Rivers and Lily Tomlin give her much credit for their success. They both say she was their role model.

Some of her many famous one-liners:

Housework won't kill you, but why take a chance?

A smile is a curve that sets everything straight.

Don't go to bed mad; stay up and fight.

MOVIE STARS AND ENTERTAINERS today don't quite seem the same as those of days past.

FINDING HOPE WHEN EVERYTHING FEELS HOPELESS

PSYCHOLOGISTS SAY IT'S [HOPE] is crucial to our physical and mental health. It guards against anxiety and despair. And it protects us from stress. Research shows that people with higher levels of hope have better coping skills and bounce back from setbacks faster. They're better at problem-solving and have lower levels of burnout. They have stronger relationships because they communicate better and are more trusting. And they are less stressed parents—more able to teach their children to set goals and solve problems.

"You can think of hope as a PPE—Personal Protective Emotion," says Anthony Scioli, a professor of psychology at Keene State College in Keene, New Hampshire, and coauthor of *Hope in the Age of Anxiety* and *The Power of Hope*.

Most psychologists define hope as a yearning for something possible but not certain—such as a better future—and a belief that you have the power to make it happen.[31]

This above article was written by Elizabeth Bernstein of *The Wall Street Journal*.

---

31   Bernstein, Elizabeth. "Finding Hope When Everything Feels Hopeless." The Wall Street Journal. October 27, 2020.

Whether we think about it or not, hope is a part of everyone's life. Everyone hopes for something. It's an inherent part of being a human being. It is a necessary ingredient for getting through tough times.[32] We all have tough times. It's part of life.

When you recover, what will you do?

When you recover, will you still be you?

Will you be stronger, will you be you?

When you recover from what you've been through?[33]

---

32 Hope Grows. "Why is hope so important?" HopeGrows.com. Accessed August 25, 2022. https://hopegrows.net/news/why-is-hope-so-important.

33 Cino, Charles A. "Now You've Recovered." Familyfriendpoems. com. Accessed September 7, 2022. https://www.familyfriendpoems. com/poem/now-youve-recovered.

BILL BRIGHT, FOUNDER OF CAMPUS CRUSADE FOR CHRIST

BILL BRIGHT, FOUNDER OF Campus Crusade for Christ, was born October 19, 1921, in Coweta, Oklahoma. He was the sixth child of the marriage. His mother's pregnancy was not going well, and the doctors encouraged her to have an abortion. The doctors were concerned that the child and possibly the mother would not survive the birth.

However, Mrs. Bright was a strong, churchgoing Christian and decided to pray to God instead. She promised God that if he would let her child live, she would dedicate her child's life to him. Bill Bright did live, but he didn't find out until many years later that his life had been dedicated to God.

Bill grew up on a ranch with his parents and grandparents. His mother and grandmother were strong, churchgoing Christians. However, his father and grandfather, even though they were highly moral men, thought church was for the womenfolk. That's the way Bill grew up.

After Bill graduated from college, he ended up in Hollywood, California. He started a food distribution company and became quite successful. As a favor to a friend he admired, he started attending the First Presbyterian Church of Hollywood. He soon joined and became very active. He also became friends with Billy Graham. He shared with Billy Graham that he would like to go into ministry full time. Billy Graham suggested to him that he get involved with college kids because there was a real need.

In 1952, Bill Bright sold his company for a substantial amount of money and used the proceeds to start Campus Crusade for Christ. His first college was UCLA. He started with four students. Today, Campus Crusade for Christ has around nineteen thousand full-time staff and around 275,000 volunteers. Campus Crusade is in over one thousand colleges worldwide in 191 countries, including Russia. Bill Bright has written over twenty books, including *The Four Spiritual Laws*, which has been translated into twenty different languages. Over two billion have been distributed.[34]

In 2001, Bill Bright's health was failing. He had pulmonary fibrosis, and the doctors gave him six months to live. Even though he was in a wheelchair, he remained very active. He actually lived another two years. During that time, he wrote a number of books and was constantly asked to speak. He later died on July 9, 2003.

He said two things that really stuck with me before he died. He said the last two years of his life were the most pro-

---

34   Campus Crusade for Christ. www.cru.org. Accessed September 7, 2022. https://www.cru.org/us/en/about.html

ductive years of his life, and if your heart is right, after adversity come great blessings.

＊＊

A FEW YEARS AGO, Jane and I were shopping at Lowe's in Franklin. The guy waiting on us was extremely nice. We could tell he was special because every time someone who worked at Lowe's would come by, they would call him by name and say something nice to him. What was different about him, though, was that he was in a wheelchair, and both his legs were missing.

I finally asked, "David, what happen to your legs?" He said, "Stupidity." I told him I didn't understand. He said that about five years ago, he was out drinking one night and had way too much to drink. He got on his motorcycle and had a terrible accident. He not only lost both his legs, but he was also paralyzed from the neck down. I said, "David, that's horrible. I feel so badly for you." He said, "Don't feel bad for me." I said, "Really? Why is that?"

He told me that at the time his son was six years old, and his daughter was six months old. However, he was not being a good father or a good husband. He wasn't even living at home. He was out drinking and running around every night. When he woke up in the hospital, his wife was standing at the end of the bed. He blurted out to her, "Why are you here? Why would you want to be here with me now?" She said, "David, I love you. I will always love you." Right then, he realized he was the luckiest man in the world.

Just about that time, the cutest little girl you would ever want to see came running in the store, jumped up in his lap, and gave him a hug and a kiss on the cheek. She then said, "Daddy, I love you." He looked at us and said, "If you don't mind, it's time for my break." They then left for the break room.

It made me think of what Bill Bright said: "If your heart is right, after adversity come great blessings."

I later learned that David was no longer working at Lowe's. He was in college working on a degree. He wanted to be a counselor involved with kids who were having problems.

DR. WILLIAM JAMES, FAMOUS PSYCHOLOGIST

DR. WILLIAM JAMES, A famous psychologist, was born in New York City in 1841. He had a rather famous family. His brother Henry James, who wrote a number of best-selling books, was probably best known for his short stories. He also wrote twelve Broadway plays. Dr. James's sister had her diary published.

Dr. James became known as the father of American psychology. At one time his books were used in most of the colleges in the United States. He said the most important discovery of his generation was that we can change our lives by changing our attitudes. This was the same thing Dr. Norman Vincent Peale said in his book, *The Power of Positive Thinking*, which became one of the best-selling books of all time.[35]

Dr. James also said that deepest principle of human nature is the craving to be appreciated. We all want to be appreciated.

A man named William was sitting in his office late one afternoon reflecting on his life. He was thinking about the people in his life who had helped him become the person he was—people who encouraged him, people who inspired him,

35   Wikipedia.org. "The Power of Positive Thinking." wikipedia.org. Accessed August 25, 2022. https://en.wikipedia.org/wiki/The_Power_of_Positive_Thinking.

people who really made a positive difference in his life. He was thinking particularly about his fifth grade teacher. So he decided to write her a letter.

Shortly after, he received a reply. The reply went like this:

> My dear William, I'm in my late eighties now, I live alone, and I'm lonely. I feel like the last leaf of autumn lingering behind. You may be interested in knowing I taught school for fifty years. Your letter is the first letter of appreciation I ever received. It came one cold, cold morning. It cheered me more than anything in many years.

WILLIAM CERTAINLY MADE A positive difference in her life. I'm sure she read that letter many, many times. But just think how William felt when he received her reply. I'm sure he read her letter many times. It probably brought tears to his eyes. When we make a positive difference in someone's life, we feel good about ourselves, and when we feel good about ourselves, life is better. When we don't feel good about ourselves, life is not as much fun. So we need to do more that makes us feel good about ourselves.

THE CUTE LITTLE KID IN THE MALL

THIS GUY WALKS IN a mall. It's a large mall—an indoor mall. As he walks in, he sees a cute little kid standing in front of one of the stores all by himself. The little kid was having a great time. He was putting his face up against the store window, making faces at people inside, twirling around, just having a great time. The little kid was totally oblivious to anything except having a great time. Even though the guy could see the kid was having a great time, he could also see he was a little too young to be left unattended.

So he decided he better check on the kid. As he gets a little close, all of a sudden, a loud voice comes over the speaker system. "Christopher Walker! Christopher Walker! Please come to the big clock in the middle of the mall. Christopher Walker, please come to the big clock in the middle of the mall." About that time, he heard the kid mutter to himself, "Rats, I must be lost again!"

We all get lost sometimes. We all get off track. We all make mistakes; we don't always use our best judgment. There are many times we would like a do-over. But you know what? So what? That's life! We shouldn't take ourselves too seriously.

I love the saying by Marie Osmond, "When we do something stupid and we are going to laugh about it later, we might as well laugh about it now." I also like the saying "He or she who learns to laugh at themselves will never cease to be entertained."

However, many people do take themselves too seriously. They carry around too many regrets, not only for what they did do but also for what they didn't. I was reading an article the other day that said 40 percent of the people in mental institutions could be out living a normal life today if somehow they could deal with their past, if somehow they could deal with their guilt.

A twelve-year-old boy named John was playing with his nine-year-old friend named Marie. Unfortunately, they found a loaded pistol in a dresser drawer, and before long little Marie was dead. The whole town turned out for the funeral—the whole town except for John. John didn't want to see anyone and refused to talk with anyone.

The morning after the funeral, Marie's older brother went next door and said to John, "John, I want to take you to school." John refused and said, "I don't ever want to see anyone again. I wish it was me that was dead." Marie's older brother insisted and finally persuaded John. He asked the principal to hold a special assembly. That morning 508 people—teachers and students—filled the assembly hall.

Marie's older brother stood them before and said these words. "My little sister was accidentally shot. It's one of those tragic things that sometimes happens in life. I want all of you to know my family and John's family went to church this morning. We took Communion." He then called John over and put his arm around him and said, "My family has forgiven John. Marie would want that. I ask all of you to forgive John. I especially ask that you help John forgive himself."

Sometimes we need to forgive others. Many times, we need to forgive ourselves.

BENJAMIN FRANKLIN

BENJAMIN FRANKLIN WAS BORN on January 17, 1706, in Boston, Massachusetts. He was the tenth son of seventeen children. Even though he was born into a poor family, he became the most educated man throughout all the colonies. He was one of—if not the most—important Founding Fathers of our nation.

He invented things like bifocals, the Franklin stove, lightning rods, swimming flippers, and the odometer. He was appointed first postmaster of Philadelphia in 1737 and the first postmaster general.

He did much research on electricity. Many of the words we use today in association with electricity are words first used by Benjamin Franklin. He coined words like *armature, condenser, battery,* and many other words.

He started the first volunteer fire department, the first library, and under his instigation, the first hospital. He was the only American to sign the Declaration of Independence, the Treaty of Alliance, the Treaty of Paris, and the Constitution of the United States.

It was Benjamin Franklin who persuaded the British, when they separated Canada from America, to give America four additional degrees of latitude in land, and as a result of that decision, America now possesses Minnesota, North Dakota, and the state of Washington.[36]

He was a writer, scientist, inventor, statesman, diplomat, printer, and publisher. He was America's first celebrity. He was inducted as an honorary member of the Swimming Hall of Fame and inducted into the Chess Hall of Fame. He started playing chess at the age of seventeen.

In 1761, he invented a glass harmonica, which was immediately embraced by composers like Mozart and Beethoven. He also invented the flexible catheter.

He created what was the first documented franchise in 1731 in Philadelphia. He entered into an arrangement with Thomas Whitmarsh to print many of his writings. As part of the agreement, Thomas Whitmarsh had to buy all of his printed materials from Benjamin Franklin.

He started *Poor Richard's Almanack* in 1732. The print runs reached ten thousand per year.[37] The contents included

36   Hintz, Eric S. "Benjamin Franklin's Inventions." Smithsonian. Updated December 16, 2016. https://invention.si.edu/benjamin-franklin-sinventions#:~:text=As%20a%20scientist%2C%20he%20was%20a%20major%20figure,including%20%E2%80%9Cbattery%2C%E2%80%9D%20%E2%80%9Cpositive%E2%80%9D%20and%20%E2%80%9Cnegative%2C%E2%80%9D%20%E2%80%9Cconductor%2C%E2%80%9D%20and%20%E2%80%9Cdischarge.%E2%80%9D.

37   Wikipedia. "Poor Richard's Almanack." Wikipedia.org. Accessed August 25, 2022. https://en.wikipedia.org/wiki/Poor_Richard%27s_Almanack.

articles on the weather, poems, sayings, astronomical and astrological information, as well as a calendar.

Some of Benjamin Franklin's more popular sayings:

Three can keep a secret if two of them are dead.

He who falls in love with himself will have no rivals.

Keep your eyes wide open before
marriage, half shut afterwards.

An investment in knowledge pays the best dividends.

He that lies down with dogs will rise with fleas.

FATHER'S DAY

IN 1909, SONORA DODD Smart was inspired by Ann Jarvis (founder of Mother's Day) to have a Father's Day. Sonora was attending one of the first official Mother's Day church services, and she started thinking of her father. If mothers deserved a day in honor of their loving service, why not fathers?

Sonora's father was a farmer and a Civil War veteran. Sonora's mother died giving birth to their youngest child in 1898. At that time Sonora was sixteen years old, and she had five younger brothers. By Sonora's account, her father performed brilliantly. "I remember everything about him," Sonora said many years later to the *Spokane Daily Chronicle*. "He was both father and mother to me and my brothers."

In 1910, Sonora brought a petition before the Spokane Ministerial Alliance to recognize the courage and devotion of all fathers like her father. She requested that the day be celebrated on June 5, her father's birthday. The local clergy liked the idea of a special Father's Day service but couldn't pull it together that quickly, so they settled on the third Sunday in June.

On that first Father's Day in 1910, church sermons across Spokane were dedicated to dear old dads. Red and white roses were passed out in honor of living and deceased fathers. The mayor of Spokane and governor of Washington issued proclamations, and Sonora found her calling. She would spend much of the next sixty years pushing for the official recognition of Father's Day as a national holiday.

Sonora won the support of her congressmen, who began to lobby for the creation of a national holiday. In 1916, President Woodrow Wilson celebrated Father's Day in Spokane during a visit to Washington. However, Father's Day would not become a national holiday until six years before Sonora's death at age ninety-six, when President Nixon signed a congressional resolution in 1972.

An unofficial Father's Day was held July 5, 1908, in Fairmont, West Virginia. The people of West Virginia were holding a memorial service to honor the 362 men killed in the Monongah mine explosion. It is the worst mine disaster in American history. The people of Fairmont, West Virginia, wanted to honor the men who died and their families. The Father's Day service was held at Century United Methodist Church by Reverend D. D. Meighen.

FATHER'S DAY POEMS

Dad, you know I like Batman,

And Superman is cool too,

But I don't really need them,

As long as I have you.

Daddy, I know your secret

That you have tried to keep suppressed,

I promise not to tell anyone,

But I know you love me the best.

Happy Father's Day, dad,

Thank you for all you have done.

If there was a reward for the best father ever,

I'm sure you would have won.

Daddy, I want you to know

How lucky mom and I are,

Because when it comes to daddies,

You really are a star.[38]

38   Homemade Gifts Made Easy. "30 Happy Father's Day Poems."
Homemadegiftsmadeeasy.com. Updated May 31, 2021. https://www.
homemade-gifts-made-easy.com/fathers-day-poems.html.

MARTHA BERRY AND BERRY COLLEGE

REPRINTED FROM NEELY YOUNG, *Georgia Made*, 2021: Martha Berry was the founder of Berry College, a liberal arts college located in Rome, Georgia. At an early age, she wanted to help children of poor tenant farmers who had no way to learn math, writing, and other basic educational skills. Her father, a wealthy merchant, was also concerned about the plight of poor farmers near their home, Oak Hill, outside Rome. She opened a high school for boys in an abandoned church to help them.

Her school started with only four students and was opened to those who were willing to study and work the land around her father's 150-acre farm that surrounded the school. Today, that first school has grown into a four-year college, with more than two thousand students and the nation's most extensive work-study program.

Her philosophy was to teach Appalachian boys and girls educational skills and modern agricultural farming training. She had a fourfold approach that included "Bible for prayer, the lamp for learning, the plow for labor, and the cabin for simplicity." She chose as the school motto, "Not to be ministered unto but to minister."

During the depression of the 1930s, times were hard for the school. Berry sent a letter to auto magnate Henry Ford asking for his support. The story goes that he sent her a dime. Discouraged, she took the dime to a feed store and purchased ten cents' worth of peanuts. The students planted the peanuts, and at the end of the season, she harvested the crop and sold it for $1,500. Martha Berry deposited the money, then wrote out a $1,500 check, which she sent to Henry Ford along with a note that read: "Mr. Ford, here is your $1,500 return for your dime invested in Berry College." She noted that the peanuts were grown by her students.

Henry Ford was so surprised that he took a train to Rome and met her. He watched her students work and study. He was so impressed that he gave her $3 million. With the donation from Henry Ford, Martha Berry was able increase her efforts for the boys' school and start a school for girls. Henry Ford gave more than $4 million to the school, and his donations encouraged to help Martha Berry raise more than $25 million. Andrew Carnegie gave her a $50,000 endowment, and other donors added to that total. President Woodrow Wilson and his wife, Ellen Axson Wilson, who was from Rome, helped her expand, but most of the school's financial support came from women's groups and small anonymous donors. Her school grew, and by 1929, it included 129 buildings on twenty-seven thousand acres.

Martha Berry became a national figure in education and was presented the Roosevelt Medal by President Calvin

Coolidge. Other honors include honorary doctorates by the University of Georgia, Duke University, and the University of North Carolina. The Georgia General Assembly honored her and she was the first woman appointed to Georgia's Board of Regents.

After she died in 1942, Martha Berry continued to receive honors. A portion of Highway 21 in Rome was named the Martha Berry Highway, and her portrait hangs in the Georgia Capitol Gallery of Distinguished Georgians. Today the college has nearly two thousand students, and 99 percent of its professors hold a PhD. The campus is called the most beautiful college in America, and *U.S. News and World Report* has named Berry University one of the best universities in the South.[39]

---

39   Young, Neely. Georgia Made: The Most Important Figures Who Shaped the State in the Twentieth Century. Charleston: The History Press, 2021.

SCHOOL DAYS

School Days, School Days, good old Golden Rule days

Readin', writin', rithmetic, taught to
the tune of a hickory stick

—Written by Will Cobb and Gus Edwards, 1907

THEY ALSO WROTE "BY the Light of the Silvery Moon," "I Can't Tell You Why I Love You but I Do," plus many more, including most of the songs in *The Wizard of the Oz*.

Bing Crosby played Gus Edwards in the 1939 film *The Star Maker*.

Gus Edwards was inducted into the Songwriters Hall of Fame in 1970.

THE STORY BEHIND THE SONG "JESUS LOVES ME"

TWO SISTERS, ANNA AND Susan Warner, were born in the 1820s. Their father was a very prominent attorney in New York City. They lived in the same home almost their entire lives, located on the banks of the Hudson River adjacent to the US Military Academy at West Point.

Unfortunately, both of their parents died when they were young and left them their home but not much money. In order to earn an income, they each started a writing career. Between the two of them, they had over seventy books published, many becoming bestsellers.

In addition to writing, Anna and Susan taught Sunday School in their home to the cadets of West Point. Every Sunday, their home would be overflowing with cadets, where they would study the Bible and sing hymns. They had such a positive influence on the cadets of West Point that when they died, they were each given a military funeral—an unprecedented move. Their home was made into a national shrine, and you can even see it today if you visit West Point.

In 1860 they wrote a book titled *Say and Seal*. *Say and Seal* became a bestseller.[40] It was about a two close friends, John Linden and Faith Derick. Among many things, John Linden taught Sunday School to the little kids in their church. One little kid was named Johnny Fax. Johnny Fax was a special little kid, and all the other kids loved him. Unfortunately, Little Johnny Fax came down with a lingering illness that would eventually take his life.

John Linden and Faith Derick made a commitment that they were going to make Little Johnny Fax's last days as happy and comfortable as they possibly could.

One afternoon when Little Johnny Fax was growing weaker and not feeling very well, he asked John Linden to pick him up, hold him, and sing to him. There were a number of popular hymns the sisters could have inserted into the book at this time. However, Anna Warner wrote a special song just for Little Johnny Fax.

No one remembers the book, and very few people remember the sisters. The song, though, is the most popular song ever sung by kids in Sunday School and Vacation Bible School.

It has four verses. All of you know the first verse; it goes like this:[41]

---

40   "Jesus Loves Me This I Know." bibilium.com. Accessed September 8, 2022. https://bibilium.com/jesus-loves-me-this-i-know-jesus-loves-me-song/.

41   Anna B. Warner, 1860 v. 2-3 by David R. McGuire ref. by William B. Bradbury, 1862.

Jesus loves me this I know

For the Bible tells me so

Little ones to Him belong

For they are weak but He is strong

Yes, Jesus loves me

TOO BAD WE DON'T know the other three verses because they deliver a very powerful message.

Jesus loves me, loves me still

Though I am weak and very ill.

That I may from sin be free,

He bled and died upon the tree.

Jesus loves me He who died,

Heaven's gate to open wide.

He will wash away my sin,

And let this little child come in.

Jesus loves me He will stay,

Close beside me all the way.

He who bled and died for me,

Now henceforth I will live for Thee.

VALENTINE'S DAY

VALENTINE'S DAY IS CELEBRATED in honor of Saint Valentine. Valentine was a Roman priest who served under the leadership of Emperor Claudius II during the third century AD. Claudius outlawed marriage for young men, thinking they made better soldiers remaining single. Saint Valentine defied Claudius and continued to perform marriages for young lovers in secret. When Valentine's actions were discovered, he was jailed for his crimes. While imprisoned, Valentine cared for his fellow prisoners and also for the jailer's blind daughter. Valentine cured the daughter's blindness, and his final act before being executed was to write her a love message signed "from your Valentine." Valentine was beheaded on AD February 14, 270.

Exchanging Valentine cards first became popular in London in the early 1800s. Esther Allen Howland is credited for bringing Valentine cards to America in 1847.[42] Shortly after graduating from college at age nineteen, she received a Valentine card from an associate of her father. At that time Valentine greeting cards were imported from Europe and not affordable for most Americans.

---

42   Meghan. "The History of the Valentines Day Card." History Cooperative. Updated February 14, 2017. Accessed September 8, 2022. https://historycooperative.org/history-valentines-day-card/.

Determined that she could make affordable cards, she convinced her father to order her the supplies she needed. She made a dozen samples and advertised through a popular magazine. She immediately received orders for over $5,000. She hired friends to help her make the cards. She was soon grossing over $100,000 a year. Today, over 145 million cards will be mailed or exchanged in the United States and over one billion worldwide.[43]

Richard Cadbury was an English entrepreneur. His father was founder of Cadbury's cocoa and chocolate company. Richard took over his father's business in 1861. He was the first to commercialize the connection of chocolates and romance. In 1868, Richard's company started producing a heart-shaped box of chocolates with cupids and rosebuds on top of the box for Valentine's Day. After the chocolates were eaten, people could use the beautiful boxes to save mementos and love letters. Today, more than thirty-six million heart-shaped boxes filled with chocolates are sold each year. That's more than fifty-eight million pounds of chocolate.

Last year, a total of 152 million roses were sold in the two weeks leading up to Valentine's Day. Eighty-seven percent of the roses sold were red. The second most popular flowers sold

43   Mass Moments. "First American Made Valentines Sold." MassMoments.org. Accessed August 25, 2022. https://www.massmoments.org/moment-details/first-american-made-valentines-sold.html.

were red carnation bouquets. There are more flowers sold leading up to Valentine's Day than any other holiday.[44]

The most popular Valentine's Day poem was written by Edmund Spenser, an English poet, in 1590. The name of the poem is "Roses Are Red, Violets Are Blue."

Smart men always remember their wives or girlfriends on Valentine's Day!

---

44   Balancing Everything. "Valentine's Day Sales Statistics." Balancingeverything.com. Accessed September 7, 2022. https://balancingeverything.com/valentines-day-sales-Statistics/.

A TOUCHING STORY

THIS HAPPENED IN THE rural South a number of years ago. A bus is bumping along a back road along the cotton fields near mostly tenant farmers' homes in Georgia. In one seat an elderly gentleman sits holding a bunch of fresh flowers very carefully. Sitting across the aisle is a shy young girl whose eyes come back again and again to the man's flowers.

The time comes for the elderly gentleman to get off. He could see the young girl continuing to look at the flowers. He impulsively hands her the flowers and says, "I can see you love the flowers. I think my wife would like for you to have them. I will tell her I gave them to you." The young girl accepts the flowers, then watches the elderly gentleman get off the bus and walk through the gate of a small cemetery.

I'm sure that had a positive effect on her life. She probably reflected many times on that incident. She may remember the man and his wife's cemetery forever. I'm also sure it made a positive difference in his life. He couldn't wait to share it with his wife.

It's positive little things that we do that make us feel good about ourselves. When we feel good about ourselves, life is better.

CHICK-FIL-A AND TRUETT CATHY

REPRINTED FROM NEELY YOUNG, *Georgia Made*, 2021: Truett Cathy is most famous for founding the Chick-fil-A restaurant chain. His first eating establishment opened in 1946 in the town of Hapeville, Georgia just south of Atlanta. He named the restaurant the Dwarf House because the building was so small. It was there in his restaurant in 1964 that Truett Cathy invented his unique chicken sandwich. The recipe called for a fried chicken breast with two pickles on a toasted bun. The dish was so popular that Cathy started other restaurants serving the dish and named his venture Chick-fil-A.

Truett Cathy had great vision. He located his Chick-fil-A restaurants inside the center of shopping malls, even before food courts were included. Eventually, Chick-fil-A were in malls all over the South, and in 1986, the company opened its first stand-alone restaurant in Atlanta.

Truett Cathy also decided to close his restaurants on Sundays. When he opened his first restaurant on a Tuesday, he found that he was tired and worn out by Sunday. A deeply religious man, he never regretted his decision to close on Sundays. He used this time teaching Sunday School for over fifty years.

To lure customers away from fast-food burger chains, Chick-fil-A produced TV, billboard, and newspaper ads using Holstein cows holding signs that said "EAT MORE

CHICKIN." The theme promoted the idea that renegade cows had trouble with spelling but were smart enough to understand self-preservation. Launched in 1995, the campaign became a hit. The company entered a partnership with the Peach Bowl, the annual football game in Atlanta. The Chick-fil-A cows reached a national audience of more than four million people.

Sales for Chick-fil-A sandwiches soared, and the company is now the largest privately owned fast-service restaurant in the country. Today there are 2,813 restaurants. Chick-fil-A has maintained its position as America's favorite restaurant for eight years in a row, according to the American Customer Satisfaction Index.

In 1984, Truett Cathy founded the WinShape Foundation to provide programs that would impact young people and families and enhance their Christian faith, character, and relationships. The foundation's mission states, "We are the Christian nonprofit known for creating space for transformation through every phase of life."

The first WinShape initiative built a foster care home at Berry College in Rome, Georgia. The home provided housing for twelve students and two foster parents. WinShape Homes now has eight foster homes established in Georgia, Alabama, and Tennessee. The foundation has also created WinShape Camps, with more than forty thousand campers each summer. Truett Cathy's vision was for them to learn leadership skills to be successful in life. Scholarships valued at up to $32,000, jointly funded by WinShape and Berry College, are awarded up to thirty students annually.

Truett Cathy received many awards over the years, including the William E. Simon Prize for Philanthropic Leadership, the Norman Vincent and Ruth Stafford Peale Humanitarian Award, the Cecil B. Day Ethics Award, and the Horatio Alger Award. He wrote several best-selling books, including *It's Easier to Succeed Than to Fail*, *Eat Mor Chickin: Inspire More People* and *It's Better to Build Boys Than Mend Men*.

Chick-fil-A has been run by the Cathy family since the restaurant chain's founding in 1946. It is currently being led by the third generation of the Cathy family.[45]

---

45   Young, Neely. Georgia Made: The Most Important Figures Who Shaped the State in the Twentieth Century. Charleston: The History Press, 2021.

THE HISTORY OF EASTER

EASTER IS A CHRISTIAN holiday that celebrates the belief in the resurrection of Jesus. The Resurrection occurred three days after Jesus was crucified by the Romans. The holiday concludes the Passion of Christ, a series of events and holidays that begins with Lent, a forty-day period of fasting, prayer, and sacrifice. It ends with Holy Week, which includes the celebration of Jesus's Last Supper with his twelve apostles. Palm Sunday begins the week before Easter and represents the day Jesus entered into Jerusalem.

The English word *Easter* takes its name from Eostre. Eostre is a goddess from Anglo-Saxon England. Eostre is the goddess of spring or renewal (new life).[46] The apostles believed that the death of Jesus and his resurrection gave us the gift of eternal and new life, meaning that those of faith will be welcomed into the kingdom of heaven.

How did eggs and rabbits become associated with Easter? The fact is that eggs, like the rabbit, have long been an ancient symbol of fertility and new life—all things associated with the springtime celebration of Easter.

---

46   All About History. "Origin of the Word Easter." allabouthistory. com. Accessed August 25, 2022. https://www.allabouthistory.org/origin-of-the-word-easter-faq.htm.

The rabbit was a symbol of new life and fertility in pre-Christian times. Its association as an Easter symbol is said to have originated in Germany, as early as the sixteenth century. German children believed if they were good, the Easter Bunny would leave them treats, sweets, and colored eggs. That was the beginning of the Easter baskets. When the Germans settled in Pennsylvania in the eighteenth century, they introduced the Easter Bunny to the United States.[47]

Germany also gets credit for the custom of the Easter egg hunt. Its origins date back to the late sixteenth century, when the Protestant reformer Martin Luther organized egg hunts for his congregation. Easter egg hunts later became a tradition in England in the nineteenth century. England was the first to introduce chocolate eggs.[48]

Here comes Peter Cottontail

Hopping down the Bunny trail

Hippity hoppity, hippity hoppity

Easter is on its way

Bringing every girl and boy

---

47   History. "Easter 2022." History.com. Updated April 7, 2022. https://www.history.com/topics/holidays/history-of-easter.

48   History. "Easter 2022." History.com. Updated April 7, 2022. https://www.history.com/topics/holidays/history-of-easter.

Baskets full of Joy

Hippity, hoppity

Happy Easter Day[49]

I REMEMBER AS A young kid, my mother would always have new Easter outfits for my sisters and me for Easter Sunday. Easter Sunday at church was always special. After church there would be an Easter egg hunt with all the families participating.

May every cloud above you

Give way to skies of blue

And on Easter morning

Let only joys shine through[50]

---

49   Autry, Gene, Steve Nelson, and Jack Rollins. "Here Comes Peter Cottontail." Decca
Records, 1950.

50   Unknown. Pinterest.com. Accessed October 13, 2022. https://www.pinterest.com/pin/69172544252968298/

WE ALL WANT TO FEEL SPECIAL

A YOUNG LADY WAS in love with two young men, and they both wanted to marry her. She couldn't make a decision. Finally, her mother said, "You need to make a decision! I kind of like Tom. Maybe you should marry Tom."

The daughter said, "I think Tom is very special. He's good looking, he's smart, and he has a great job."

"Well, are you going to marry Tom?"

"No, I'm going to marry Joe."

"If you feel Tom is so special, why are you marrying Joe?"

"Because Joe makes me feel special."

We all want to feel special.

***

DALE CARNEGIE WROTE THE book How to Win Friends and Influence People. It is one of the best-selling books of all time. It was published in 1936 and has sold over thirty million copies. It is ranked by the Library of Congress as the seventh most influential book in American history. It's printed in forty-five different languages.[51]

Dale Carnegie started conducting business courses in New York in 1912. Today, Dale Carnegie, Inc. has training offices in seventy countries with over five million graduates. Just to name a few—Ronald Reagan, Warren Buffett, Lyndon B. Johnson, Ann Landers, Lou Holtz, Joe DiMaggio, Mary Kay Ash, and many more.

Dale Carnegie said, "When someone cares enough to pay attention to us, it never fails to make us feel just a tad bit special." Keep in mind, when someone makes us feel special, we in turn also feel special about them.

Dale Carnegie also said, "You can make more friends in two months by being interested in them than in two years by making them interested in you."[52] Many times, people don't want an entertaining conversationalist partner; they just want someone to listen.

---

51   Wikipedia. "How to Win Friends and Influence People." Wikipedia.org. Accessed August 25, 2022. https://en.wikipedia.org/wiki/How_to_Win_Friends_and_Influence_People.

52   Carnegie, Dale. How to Win Friends and Influence People. New York: Simon and Schuster, 1936.

DALE CARNEGIE QUOTES

Those convinced against their will are
of the same opinion still.

If you want to gather honey, don't kick over the beehive.

Do the hard jobs first. The easy jobs
will take care of themselves.

The royal road to a man's heart is to talk to
him about the things he treasures most.

I WAS INTRODUCED TO a nice lady about a month ago at a local function. I immediately began asking her questions about herself and her pet projects. She was quite interesting. Later she told one of her friends how interesting I was. I never said a word. All I did was ask her a few questions. I guess I was just being a good listener.

THE PERFECT FRIEND

A friend is someone to turn to

when our spirits need a lift

a friend is someone we treasure

for true friendship is a gift

a friend is someone we laugh with

over little personal things

a friend is someone we're serious with

in facing whatever life brings

a friend is someone who fills our lives

with beauty joy and grace

and makes the world that we live in

a better and happier place[53]

53   Rios, Valerie S. "The Perfect Friend." Updated October 2007.
https://www.familyfriendpoems.com/poem/greeting-card-friend-
ship-poem.

THE GIFT OF A SMILE

Laugh and the Whole World Laughs with You;

Weep and You Weep Alone

THESE LINES FIRST APPEARED in "Solitude," a poem written in the February 25, 1882, issue of the *New York Sun*. The author was Ella Wheeler, who received five dollars for her work.[54]

It's important to laugh, but it is also important to smile. Studies have proven there are a number of reasons we should smile.[55] Just to name a few:

Perhaps the most compelling reason to smile is that it may lengthen your lifespan. Studies have shown that genuine, intense smiling is associated with a longer life.

---

54   Trivia Library. "Origins of Sayings." TriviaLibrary.com. Accessed August 25, 2022. https://trivia-library.com/b/origins-of-sayings-laugh-and-the-world-laughs-with-you.htm.

55   Divine You. "8 Health Benefits of Smiling Proven by Science." DivineYouWellness.com. Accessed August 25, 2022. https://divineyouwellness.com/blog/benefits-of-smiling/#:~:text=%208%20Health%20Benefits%20of%20Smiling%20%201,when%20a%20person%20smiles.%20Subsequently%2C%20the...%20More%20.

Smiling reduces stress. Believe it or not, smiling reduces stress, even if you don't feel like smiling or even if you fake it.

Smiling elevates mood. Next time you are feeling down, try putting on a smile. A simple smile can trigger the release of neuropeptides, which can boost your mood.

Smiling is contagious. Smiling not only has the ability to elevate your mood, but it can change the moods of others for the better.

Smiling boosts the immune system. Studies have shown that when you smile, immune function improves because you are more relaxed (thanks to the release of certain transmitters).

A smile with love behind it has so many positive effects on us; it stimulates the brain, makes you come across as friendly, and brings joy to those around you. Whether you say hello to a stranger you pass in the grocery store or wave to your neighbor on the run, adding a smile to these simple acts of kindness can make someone's day go from drab to fab. Try it. It works.

A smile will do so many things,

It seems almost divine;

I wish they all had angel wings,

And everywhere could shine

A smile is cheer to you and me

The cost is nothing—it's given free

It comforts the weary—gladdens the sad

Consoles those in trouble—good and bad

To rich and poor—beggar or thief

It's free to all of any belief.

A natural gesture of young and old

Cheers on the faint—disarms the bold

Unlike most blessings for which we pray

It's one thing we keep when we give away[56]

A SMILE IS A very inexpensive way to improve your looks instantly.

If you see someone without a smile, give them one of yours. It will make a positive difference in both parties.

Don't forget to smile; it builds trust. however, some may wonder what you are up to.

One of my favorite quotes:

---

56   Poole, William C. "What a Smile Will Do." Public domain.

Don't judge each day by the Harvest you
reap but by the seeds you plant.

—Robert Louis Stevenson, Treasure Island, 1882

HAPPINESS

WE OFTEN BELIEVE HAPPINESS, money, and fame go together. This is not always true. Actually, recent studies have shown that the more someone is in the spotlight and the more money someone has, the more likely that someone will suffer from anxiety and depression and be more likely to commit suicide.[57]

Bobby Darin was born May 14, 1936. He started his career as a songwriter for Connie Francis. He recorded his first million-selling single, "Splish Splash," in 1958. He was also the cowriter. He won the Golden Glove Award in his first film, *Come September*. In 1960, he was given the Grammy Award for record of the year, *Mack the Knife*, and he was also named Artist of the Year. He wrote the song "Danke Schoen" and gave it to his good friend Wayne Newton. This song launched Wayne's career.

When he was thirty-one years old, Darin discovered that the woman who raised him was his grandmother, not his mother as he had thought. The woman whom he had thought

---

57   Gaba, Sherry. "Fame, Mania and Depression: The Hidden Link." BeliefNet.com. Accessed August 25, 2022. https://www.beliefnet.com/columnists/thecelebritytherapist/2013/10/fame-mania-and-depression-the-hiddenlink.html#:~:text=In%20a%20very%20recent%20study%20published%20in%202013%2C,a%20significant%20number%20that%20have%20it%20in%20common.

was his sister was his mother. Those events deeply affected him and sent him into a long period of depression.

In 1957 he had a son out of wedlock. Later that year he married Sandra Dee. They divorced in 1967. He died at age thirty-seven.

Sandra Dee was born May 14, 1940. She started her career as a child model at age four. She was fourteen when she signed a contract for the movie *Until They Sail*. She was best known for her performances in *Imitation of Life* and *Gidget*, both in 1959. In 1960, her career began to decline. She suffered from anorexia, drug abuse, heavy smoking, and alcohol abuse. She also suffered from sexual abuse by her stepfather during her teens. She died at age sixty-two.

Ashley Judd spent forty-seven days at a treatment center for depression in 2006. "I needed help," she told *Glamour* magazine. "I was in so much pain."

Lady Gaga says she has dealt with depression and anxiety her whole life.

Bruce "the Boss" Springsteen had bouts of depression in his sixties. "It's like this thing that engulfs you. I got where I didn't want to get out of bed."

Just to name a few out of many who committed suicide or died as a result of drug abuse: Robin Williams, Alan Ladd, George Reeves (*Superman*), Ernest Hemingway, Brian Keith, Montgomery Clift (died of heart attack due to drug and alcohol abuse), River Phoenix (drug overdose at age twenty-three).

There is a Chinese saying that goes: "If you want happiness for an hour, take a nap. If you want happiness for a day, go fishing. If you want happiness for a year, inherit a fortune. If you want happiness for a lifetime, help somebody." For centuries, the greatest thinkers have suggested the same thing: happiness is found in helping others.

For it is in giving that we receive.

—Saint Francis of Assisi

The whole meaning of life is to serve humanity.

—Leo Tolstoy

We make a living by what we get; we
make a life by what we give.

—Winston Churchill

Making money is happiness; making other
people happy is super Happiness.

—Nobel Laureate Professor Muhammad Yunus

Happiness is like a butterfly, the more you chase it, the
more it will elude, but if you turn your attention to other
things, it will come and sit softly on your shoulder."

—Henry David Thoreau, 1848

Remember: It is always the journey. It is not the destination.

"The Station," by Robert J. Hastings

TUCKED AWAY IN OUR subconscious is an idyllic vision. We
will soon reach the station. How restlessly we are waiting, wait-
ing for the station. When we finally reach the station, we cry!
That will be it. When I'm 18. When I buy that new Mercedes.
When I put my last kid through college. When I pay off the
mortgage. Then I will live happily ever after.

The truth is, there is no station. It's the trip. It's the journey. Relish the moment. Stop waiting. Instead, eat more ice cream, go barefoot more often, swim in more rivers, laugh more, cry less, climb more mountains, spend more time with your family and friends. Start today.

MEMORIAL DAY

MEMORIAL DAY IS THE day to remember and honor with gratitude all those who served and died for our country to protect our freedom. We must never forget; freedom is not free. Someone has to pay, and many, many have.

A number of cities and towns in the South claim to be the first to celebrate Memorial Day. However, Memorial Day first started in Boalsburg, Pennsylvania, in 1864, immediately after the Battle of Gettysburg. A large group of ladies put flowers on the graves of the soldiers killed in the Battle of Gettysburg.[58]

The Battle of Gettysburg was the largest battle in the Civil War. Over ten thousand men were killed, and over forty thousand were injured. That was the battle that cost the Confederacy the war. There were more than 620,000 men killed, more than any other war, even World War II.[59] It was a horrible war. America was split. Families were split—sometimes brother against brother. My great-grandfather on one side of

---

58   Historic Boalsburg. "Memorial Day." HistoricBoalsburg.com. Accessed August 25, 2022. https://historicboalsburg.com/things-to-do/memorial-day/.

59   History Net. "The Battle of Gettysburg: Facts & Info About a Turning Point in the Civil War." Historynet.com. Accessed August 2, 2022. https://www.historynet.com/battle-of-Gettysburg/.

our family fought for the North. My great-grandfather on the other side of the family fought for the South.

North Carolina was about evenly split. Some were for the North, and some were for the South. Finally, North Carolina reluctantly joined the Confederacy. They didn't have much choice. They were surrounded by Georgia, South Carolina, Tennessee, and Virginia. However, many still fought for the North.

In 1865, after Boalsburg, a group of women from Vicksburg, Mississippi, decorated the graves of soldiers buried in the Vicksburg cemetery. Later that same year, women in Columbus, Mississippi, put flowers on the graves of both Union and Confederate soldiers. Soon towns across America, North and South, were honoring soldiers killed in the Civil War.

Rochester, Wisconsin, was the first town to celebrate Memorial Day with a Memorial Day parade in 1867.

On May 5, 1868, General John A. Logan, commander of the Grand Army of the Republic, an organization of Union veterans, declared May 30 to be the official date for Memorial Day. But for fifty years, the South refused to celebrate Memorial Day the same day as the North. As you may imagine, there was much bitterness on both sides. How do you forgive someone who killed a member of your family? It's hard. And I'm sure some people never forgave. There were two Methodist churches in Highlands in the late 1800s—a Northern Methodist and a Southern Methodist. Finally, in 1904 they merged and built the church we have today.

**

IN 1918, IMMEDIATELY AFTER the end of World War I, Congress passed a law to make Memorial Day not only Memorial Day for the Civil War but for all wars. They declared it would be observed on May 30. From 1868 to 1971, Memorial Day was always celebrated on May 30 of each year. In 1971, it was changed to the last Monday in May. Congress wanted it to be an official holiday and a three-day weekend.

And that is how Memorial Day got started in America.

Some people say there are not enough heroes today. I say they don't know where to look. At one time there were over 91,000 risking their lives in Afghanistan and Iraq. Even today there are still over five thousand.[60] They are heroes.

Martin A. Treptow grew up in Chippewa Falls, Wisconsin. Later, he was a barber in Cherokee, Iowa. In 1917, he volunteered to serve in World War I. He was attached to the Forty-Second Rainbow Division. They were in France under heavy fire from the Germans. He volunteered to carry a message from his platoon to another platoon and was killed. Later they found on his body his diary, in which he inscribed the

---

60   Associated Press. "A timeline of the US military presence in Afghanistan." APNews.com. Updated September 8, 2019. https://apnews.com/article/fd2ec2085b0b4fd3ae0a3b03c6de9478.

following pledge: "America must win this war. Therefore, I will work, I will save, I will sacrifice, I will endure, I will fight cheerfully and do my utmost as if the whole issue of the struggle depended on me alone."

Martin A. Treptow is buried in Bloomer, Wisconsin. He was twenty-four years old. Martin A. Treptow was certainly a hero.

JULY FOURTH IN AMERICA

JULY FOURTH IS ALSO known as Independence Day. It's the day America celebrates independence from Great Britain. It was actually declared July 2, 1776, by the Continental Congress. However, it wasn't until two days later, July 4, 1776, that the Declaration of Independence was revised and signed. That was 246 years ago.

The thirteen colonies wanted freedom from England's control and high taxes. This led to the beginning of the Revolutionary War. The Revolutionary War was led by General George Washington. It started on April 19, 1775. It officially ended on September 3, 1783.

Thomas Jefferson was the main author of the Declaration of Independence. John Hancock was the first to sign the Declaration of Independence. His bold signature is where we get the phase "put your John Hancock here" when asked to sign your name.

John Adams always claimed July 2, 1776, to be the official day of independence. He wrote a letter to his wife, Abigail, telling her that Independence Day would be celebrated forever with parades, bonfires, and fireworks. How right he was. Abigail Adams is best known for her now-famous admonition that the Founding Fathers "remember the ladies" in their new laws.

She opposed slavery and was a strong supporter of women's education.

Philadelphia, Pennsylvania, held the first annual commemoration of independence on July 4, 1777. The first Fourth of July parade was held in Bristol, Rhode Island, on July 4, 1785. Philadelphia also rings the Liberty Bell thirteen times every July fourth at 2:00 p.m. in honor of the thirteen colonies.

The Evening Pennsylvania Post was the first American daily newspaper and the first to print the US Declaration of Independence July 4, 1783.

Three presidents who signed the Declaration of Independence died on July 4. John Adams and Thomas Jefferson both died on July 4, 1826. James Monroe died on July 4, 1831. Calvin Coolidge is the only president to be born on July 4.

Macy's fireworks show in New York City uses more than seventy-five thousand fireworks shells and costs about $6 million. There are usually about sixteen thousand July fourth firework displays that happen around the country.[61]

---

61   Cohen, Michelle. "Macy's fireworks by the numbers." Pyrospec. com. June 29, 2018.
https://www.pyrospec.com/macys-2018-by-the-numbers/#:~:-
text=More%20fun%20facts%20The%20first%20big%20Ma-
cy%E2%80%99s%20fireworks,Walt%20Disney%20Company%20to%20
celebrate%20the%20nation%E2%80%99s%20Bicentennial.

According to the National Beer Wholesalers Association, there are more beer sales on the Fourth of July than any other day in America.[62]

Nathan's Famous Hot Dog Eating Contest is held annually on July fourth. The record is held by Joey Chestnut. Joey ate seventy-six hot dogs with buns in just ten minutes in 2022. Also, there are more hot dogs eaten on the Fourth of July than any other day—typically, more than 150 million.[63]

62   NBWA. "Industry Fast Facts." NBWA.org. Accessed August 25, 2022.
https://www.nbwa.org/resources/industry-fast-facts.

63   Wikipedia. "Joey Chestnut." Wikipedia.org. Accessed August 25, 2022.
https://en.wikipedia.org/wiki/Joey_Chestnut.

THE POWER OF GRATITUDE

THE POWER OF GRATITUDE is something I recently learned that is so important in everyone's life. It is certainly making a positive difference in my life. The power of gratitude is so simple, yet it is so powerful. The benefits are unlimited. I wish someone had shared with me the importance of the power of gratitude when I was young. It would have made a big difference in my life. I would have been a better person. Plus, the power of gratitude has been scientifically proven to work every time with anyone that will use it.

Just to name a few benefits: It will increase your joy and passion in life, elevate your feelings of self-worth, lift your mood, halve your risk of depression, create more positive feelings and emotions, reduce anxiety and stress, lower blood pressure, promote forgiveness, strengthen relationships, strengthen your immune system, and provide overall better health and, for many, a better night's sleep.[64] The benefits go on and on and on.

It is impossible to feel grateful and depressed at the same moment. Over two hundred suicidal patients with severe de-

---

64   Miller, Kori D. "14 Health Benefits of Practicing Gratitude According to Science."
PositivePsychology.com. Updated June 18, 2019. https://positivepsychology.com/benefits-of-gratitude/#benefits.

pression problems were asked to write down everything they were grateful for. The results were amazing. Ninety percent had positive improvement, and many are living more positive lives today. It has also proven to be effective in treating people with addiction problems and people with mental problems. It is especially effective with people with depression problems.[65]

It has not only been scientifically proven, but it is also confirmed by the Bible. There are hundreds of verses that tell us to thank God for our many blessings. Two of my favorites are: "In everything give thanks; for this is the will of God for us through Christ Jesus" (1 Thessalonians 5:18(KJV) and "O Lord, I will give thanks to you with all my heart, I will tell of your wonderful deeds" (Psalm 9:1(NIV),

Willie Nelson said, "When I started counting my blessings, my whole life turned around."

Zig Ziglar said, "The greatest source of happiness is the ability to be grateful at all times"

Cicero, Rome's greatest orator and statesman, said in 70 BC, "Gratitude is not only the greatest of all virtues but the parent of all others. It unlocks the fullness of life."

I started a gratitude journal. Every day I write down three to five things I notice that I'm grateful for. It doesn't have to be overwhelming—maybe seeing a baby's smile, a beautiful

---

65   Schor, Jacob. "Gratitude Diary Improves Mood in Suicidal Inpatients." Natural Medicine Journal. Updated September 4, 2019. https://www.naturalmedicinejournal.com/journal/gratitude-diary-im-proves-mood-suicidal-inpatients.

sunset, a rainbow after a storm, the majestic white pelicans passing through Orlando in our beautiful lakes, having lunch with friends, a phone call from a grandchild. The other day I got caught on I-4 because of an auto accident. This time I was grateful I wasn't the one in the accident. It's counting one's blessings opposed to life's annoyances. It's a choice.

There is an article in *Forbes* magazine by Erika Anderson titled "How Feeling Grateful Can Make You More Successful."[66] Try it. It works. The more you look for things to be grateful for, the more you will find. It will soon become a way of life. It will soon be a habit.

At the University of California at Berkeley, their science center's studies[67] show that practicing gratitude can not only increase happiness but also allow one to lead a more meaningful life and experience a better world. The practice of gratitude has unlimited benefits.

Finally, the positive psychology movement has recognized gratitude as maybe the most important strength and virtue which enables a person to live well and as the "sweetest

---

66   Anderson, Erika. "How Feeling Grateful Can Make You More Successful." Forbes.com. Updated November 27, 2013. https://www.forbes.com/sites/erikaandersen/2013/11/27/how-feeling-grateful-can-make-you-more-successful/?sh=1394d6312de7.

67   Brown, Joshua, and Joel Wong. "How Gratitude Changes You and Your Brain."
GreaterGoodMagazine.com. Updated June 6, 2017. https://greatergood.berkeley.edu/
article/item/how_gratitude_changes_you_and_your_brain.

emotion" of all the emotions. Gratitude may have the highest connection to mental health and happiness of any of the personality traits ever studied. It turns what we have into enough and more. It turns denial into acceptance, chaos into order, and confusion into clarity. It can turn a meal into a feast, a house into a home, a stranger into a friend.

> Be thankful for what you have, you'll end up
> having more. If you concentrate on what you
> don't have, you will never have enough.

—Oprah Winfrey

GRATITUDE IS ONE OF the sweet shortcuts to finding peace and happiness. It is one of the most medicinal emotions we can feel.

It is impossible to be depressed and grateful at the same time.

P.S. Keep a gratitude journal, and when a day comes along that you don't quite feel up to par, go back and read what you wrote down previous days. I promise it will lift your mood; it will make a positive difference.

MEMORIAL DAY AND
THE POPPY RED

THE POPPY RED IS a flower that grows wild in the fields of Belgium. The Poppy Red was made famous by a poem written in 1915 called "Flanders Fields." "Flanders Fields" was written by a young colonel, John McCrae, a medical doctor in the Canadian Army. It was written immediately after a horrible seventeen all-day and all-night battle in which most of the young Canadian soldiers were killed. The setting was Flanders Fields, Belgium, where wild poppies grew.

In 1918, a young American girl, Moina Michael, wrote a poem in response to "Flanders Fields." Her poem went like this:

We too honor the Poppy Red;

It grows in a field where valor led;

It seems to signal to the sky,

That the blood of heroes will never die.[68]

---

68   Michael, Moina. "We Shall Keep The Faith." Wikipedia.org. Accessed August 25, 2022. https://en.wikipedia.org/wiki/We_Shall_Keep_the_Faith.

This young lady, Moina Michael, was the first person to wear a Poppy Red on Memorial Day. She got her friends to wear a Poppy Red on Memorial Day, and they started selling Poppy Reds to raise money for the disabled veterans. At one time there were millions of Americans wearing a Poppy Red on Memorial Day.

In 1923, the Veterans of Foreign Wars (VFW) started selling Poppy Reds to raise money for the disabled veterans of World War I. Funds were raised for the rehabilitation and employment of disabled servicemen in honor of Memorial Day.

The Poppy Red also became popular in parts of Europe. There was a lady visiting from France who was so impressed that she went back home and soon started selling Poppy Reds to raise money for the widows and orphans of World War I in honor of their Memorial Day.

In 1948, the United States Post Office had a first-class stamp in of honor Moina Michael for what she did for Memorial Day in America.

Some of you may remember the Poppy Red. I know many of your parents and grandparents knew all about the Poppy Red. My mother always wore a Poppy Red on Memorial Day.

* * *

MOINA BELLE MICHAEL WAS born in Good Hope, Georgia, on August 15, 1869. Her father, John Marion Michael, fought for the South in the Civil War. Her uncle on her father's side,

General Francis Marion, fought in the American Revolution-ary War (1775–1783). He was known as the "Swamp Fox." On her mother's side, her uncle, John Wise, was governor of Virginia.

Moina Michael was a professor at the University of Georgia. She received a number of awards. In 1944, a liberty ship in World War II was named SS *Moina Michael* in her honor. In 1969, the Georgia General Assembly named a section of US Highway 78 the Moina Michael Highway. In 1999, she was named to the Georgia Women Achievement Hall of Fame. She was a member of the Daughters of the American Revolution and the United Daughters of the Confederacy.

RALPH WALDO EMERSON

RALPH WALDO EMERSON IS one of the most important and most influential figures in the history of America. His thoughts, writings, lectures, poems, and books continue to influence us over a hundred years after his death. He not only influenced countless ordinary people but political leaders, intellectuals, and prominent writers throughout the world.

After graduating from Harvard number one in his class, he later started making a living as a public speaker. He became very popular giving his thoughts on current events and philosophical topics. He published his first book of essays in 1841 and published a second volume in 1842.

Even today we are continually influenced in American literature by Ralph Waldo Emerson's profound essays, poems, quotes, and classic books. *Self-Reliance* is one of his most influential books. His works are still being read and discussed more than 150 years after his death.

A few of his quotes:

To laugh often and much: To win the respect of intelligent people and the affection of children, to earn the appreciation of honest critics and endure the betrayal of false friends, to appreciate beauty, to find the best in others, to leave the world a bit better whether by a healthy child, a garden patch, or redeemed social condition; to know even one life has breathed easier because you lived. This is to have succeeded.

Our greatest glory is not in never failing,
but in rising up every time we fail.

Live in the sunshine, swim the sea, drink the wild air.

Without ambition one starts nothing.

Nothing great was ever achieved without enthusiasm.

Life is a journey not a destination.

To be yourself in a world that is constantly trying to make you something else is the greatest accomplishment.

For every minute you are angry, you
lose 60 seconds of happiness.

Finish each day and be done with it.

It is one of the most beautiful compensations
of life, that no man can sincerely try to help
another without helping himself.

QUOTES TO LIVE BY

It is one of the most beautiful compensations
of this life that no man can sincerely try to
help another without helping himself.

—Ralph Waldo Emerson

Well-adjusted means you can make the same
mistake over and over again, and keep smiling.

—George Bergman

The more sympathy you give, the less you need.

—Malcolm Forbes

When someone sings his own praises, he
always gets the tune too high.

—Mary Waldrip

Trust is the most important element in building relationships.

—Unknown

Don't let what you cannot do influence what you can do.

—John Wooden

Communication—many times less is more.

—Unknown

When you are good at something, you'll tell everyone.
When you are great at something, they'll tell you.

—Walter Peyton

The highest reward for a person's toil is not what
they get for it but what they become by it.

—John Ruskin

Always look at what you have left. Never
look at what you have lost.

—Robert Schuller

One thing that's good about procrastination is that
you always have something planned for tomorrow.

—Gladys Bronwyn Stern

Jealousy is the tribute mediocrity pays to genius.

—Fulton J. Sheen

The nice thing about egoists is they
don't talk about other people.

—Lucille S. Harper

What we see as negatives in our eyes are
often God's blessings in disguise.

—Unknown

Get someone else to blow your horn and
the sound will travel twice as far.

—Will Rogers

The more interesting the gossip, the
more likely it is to be untrue.

—Unknown

Tact is rubbing out another's mistake instead of rubbing it in.

—Leo Buscaglia

In spite of the cost of living, it's still popular.

—Kathleen Norris

Don't judge each day by the Harvest you
reap but by the seeds you plant.

—Robert Louis Stevenson

You'll never be completely sure of your opinion until
you talk to someone with the opposite opinion.

—Sandy Seay

Let us always meet each other with a smile,
for the smile is the beginning of love.

—Mother Teresa

SING SOFTLY

Sing softly to yourself today

No matter what the tune

And maybe joy will find you

And maybe, really soon

For songs can open up our hearts

And likewise ears and eyes,

And sometimes we are treated

To a Saturday surprise.

And whether sung or hummed

A tune can bring a smile,

Recalling cherished memories not remembered for a while.

No matter the bucket size

Your tune is carried in,

Your song is worth the effort

So let us now begin.

Sing softly to yourself today

No one needs to hear,

But maybe your soft singing

Will draw the Spirit near.

And as you walk your way today

On paths both short and long,

remember if you want to sing

You can always find a song.

— Rev. Randy Lucas, Highlands United Methodist
Church, Highlands, North Carolina

HELPING OTHERS

ONE OF MY VERY close friends grew up in a little South Carolina town - Typical, small-town America. He graduated from the University of South Carolina and after college he was an officer in the Air Force. Later, he had a successful business career in Orlando, Florida. He is a man of integrity and a Christian.

Occasionally, he gives to charities like The American Heart Association and The American Cancer Society. But he has never really felt the need to give to charities that support the poor and people with financial problems. His feelings have always been - if they worked hard like he did, they wouldn't have any financial problems. He's a nice guy, a great friend and I'm sure all of you would like him.

One day he happened to catch Joel Osteen on TV. Joel Osteen was preaching on giving, the benefits of giving and how the Bible has over 300 verses that pertain to giving and helping the poor. Joel Osteen said that many, many times both lives are changed - the person receiving the gift is changed and the person giving the gift is changed. Joel Osteen told one story of a lady that helps a poor black kid whose family has a hard time putting enough food on the table. Later, the kid becomes a doctor. Years later, the lady ends up going in a hospital for an operation she cannot afford. She does not recognize the doctor, but he recognizes her. He pays her hospital bill.

This story impresses my friend. He begins to look at helping others that need help in a different way.

The next day while he is getting a haircut, he says to the lady cutting his hair that his birthday is coming up and he is going next door to treat himself to a manicure and pedicure. She thinks that is a great idea. Everyone should treat themselves to something special once in a while, especially on their birthday.

He then asked her if she ever gets a manicure and pedicure herself. "Oh no" she says. "I'm a single parent with 10-year-old twin daughters. We struggle every month just to make ends meet. Manicures and pedicures are not in our budget. After he gets his manicure and pedicure, he buys a gift certificate for a manicure and pedicure. He then goes back and gives it to her. She starts crying. She is overwhelmed; he is overwhelmed. He tears up.

Later that afternoon he and I are hitting golf balls. He can't wait to tell me the story. He tells me all the details about what Joel Osteen says. I've never seen him so passionate. Maybe both of their lives will be changed.

The point is, when we do something special, when we help someone in need, when we make a positive difference in someone's life, when we contribute to a worthy cause, we feel good about ourselves. When we feel good about ourselves, life is better. When we don't feel good about ourselves, life is not as much fun. We need to do more things that help us feel good about ourselves.

Proverbs 22:9(NRSV) "Those who are generous are blessed"

I WALKED A MILE WITH PLEASURE

"I walked a mile with Pleasure;

She chatted all the way;

But left me none the wiser

For all she had to say.

I walked a mile with Sorrow;

And ne'er a word said she;

Bu,t oh! The things I learned from her,

When Sorrow walked with me."[69]

— Robert Browning Hamilton

69   Hamilton, Robert Browing. "I Walked a Mile with Pleasure." Go-odreads.com. Accessed October 13, 2022. https://www.goodreads.com/quotes/289683-i-walked-a-mile-with-pleasure-she-chatted-all-the

LITTLE THINGS

A summer's breeze, a baby's smile

A daffodil that's growing wild

A deep orange sunset in the west

Those little things, I love the best

A still dark night with fireflies

The laughter in my mother's eyes

A multicolored rainbow's end

Are little things that count, my friend

A fuzzy warm puppy licking my face

Kisses with hugs and a loving embrace

Rain pouring down on a roof made of tin

Sitting under a shade with a soft gentle wind

Those little things make life worth living

Being kind to a stranger, caring and giving

Laughing And sharing your hopes and your dreams

There is nothing more precious than those little things[70]

---

70   Unknown

CHURCH AND COFFEE

I WANT TO SHARE with you the connection of the church and coffee. Everyone is familiar with coffee. Most of you probably drink coffee. But you may not know how big coffee really is. Coffee is the world's second largest commodity next to the petroleum industry. It is the most popular hot drink in the world – over 2 billion cups of coffee are consumed every day. When you think about coffee, you usually think about Columbia. But Brazil is by far the number one country in the production of coffee.

The first coffee house was in Constantinople in 1475. Coffee was first introduced in America in Jamestown, Virginia by Captain John Smith in 1607. The first coffee house in England was in 1642. You also may be interested to know the famous insurance company, Lloyds of London started out as a coffee house in 1668.

Lloyds of London coffee house was also where people first started tipping - you know tipping the waitresses and waiters. They had a sign that had the letters T.I.P.S. and people tipped before they were served, making sure they would be served promptly and properly.

The first espresso machine was invented in Paris, France in 1842. But it really became popular in Italy. Today, there are over 200,000 espresso bars in Italy.

Maxwell House Coffee had its start in 1882 and was named after a hotel in Nashville, Tennessee. At one time, Maxwell House coffee was the number one selling coffee in the United States. In 1907, President Theodore Roosevelt was visiting Nashville, and was staying at the Maxwell House Hotel. He was served his very first cup of Maxwell House coffee. After finishing his cup, he was asked if he would like another. He replied, "Yes indeed, indeed I would. It's good to the last drop." And that's how Maxwell House coffee came up with their famous slogan, "Maxwell House coffee, it's good to the last drop." In 1942, every American soldier had a packet of instant Maxwell House coffee in their ration kit.

In 1948, Dunkin Donuts opened their first store in Quincy, Massachusetts. Today they have over 12,000 locations and operate in 45 different countries. Over 60% of their revenue comes from coffee, not from donuts.

In 1972, Starbucks opened their first store in Seattle, Washington. Today, they have 34,000 locations and operate in 76 different countries. In a single month, Starbucks had over $2 billion in revenue.

You may be interested to know how Starbucks decided on naming their company. It was a big decision, and a number of different names were suggested. Finally, Gordon Bowker and Terry Heckler, 2 founders of Starbucks were both familiar with Herman Melville's novel Moby-Dick. They made the decision that Starbuck, the first mate on the ship in the novel evoked the romance of the high seas and the seafaring tradition of the early coffee traders. Thus, the name Starbucks was adopted.

Just as a side note, Moby Dick is based on a true story. It is considered to be the first American classic novel. In 1852, it was the best-selling book in America, after the Bible.

This is all interesting but what does it have to with the church?

In 850 A.D., a goat herder from Ethiopia noticed that when his goats were in a certain field, they seemed to have more energy and were harder to manage. After doing some investigating, he discovered that in this one particular field, they were eating beans on a tree. He tried the beans. They made him more energetic and more alert. He started sharing the beans with his friends. They started boiling them in water and that is the beginning of coffee in 850 A.D in Ethiopia.

In the early 1500's, Pope Vincent III was the Pope of Italy. As coffee began to get popular in Italy, some of the people went to Pope Vincent III and asked him to ban coffee. They said it was a drink of the devil. But it was too late. Pope Vincent III was already drinking coffee and he loved it. He told the people it was really a drink from God because it helped to keep the monks awake during long prayers.

So, Pope Vincent III blessed coffee and coffee began to flourish in Italy. Today coffee is the most popular hot drink in the world.

"I WILL ALWAYS LOVE YOU"

"I Will Always Love You," was written and recorded by Dolly Parton in 1973. It was a number one hit in 1973 on the Billboard Hot Country charts and again when it was recorded for the 1982 soundtrack, *The Best Little Whorehouse in Texas*.

However, Whitney Houston's version, recorded in 1992 for the film *The Bodyguard*, holds the record for being the best-selling single for a woman in music history. Dolly has received over $5 million in royalties from Whitney Houston's version. Dolly Parton has said many times, "Nobody can sing it like Whitney."

"I Will Always Love You" is not a conventional love song. Dolly was invited by country star Porter Wagoner to co-host his TV show, where they became famous for their duets.

However, her huge talent soon eclipsed her appreciation for their time together and she chose to leave his show. Porter Wagoner thought her leaving was a mistake and that she was being disloyal to him. She played the song for him the morning after she wrote it, as her way of letting him know she had made her decision, and to show him just how she felt about him.

Dolly later said Porter Wagoner was in tears when she finished, and he called it "the prettiest song he ever heard." I wrote that song to say, "Here's how I feel, I will always love you, but I have to go"

If I should stay

I would only be in your way

So I'll go but I know

I'll think of you every step of the way[71]

---

71   Wikipedia. "I Will Always Love You." Wikipedia.org. Accessed
August 28, 2022. https://en.wikipedia.org/wiki/I_Will_Always_Love_
You

ACKNOWLEDGMENTS

I HOPE YOU FIND these articles to be inspiring, uplifting, and heartwarming. Most of all, I hope they make a positive difference in your life. When we make a positive difference in someone's life, we feel good about ourselves. And when we feel good about ourselves, life is simply better.

I've always found gratitude to be one of the most important aspects of a positive and successful life. It's widely acknowledged that gratitude is a core strength that enables an individual to live well. As the great motivational speaker Zig Ziglar summed up, "The greatest source of happiness is the ability to be grateful at all times." Interestingly, it is virtually impossible to be grateful and depressed at the same time.

In a classic experiment, two hundred suicidal patients were asked to write down everything they were grateful for. The results were amazing. Ninety percent showed immediate improvement, and many are living a more positive life today.[59]

Try this and see for yourself: At the end of every day, write down four or five things that happened to you during the day that you're grateful for. Do this every day, and I guarantee it will make a positive difference in your life.

Of the many people in my life I am grateful for, I would like to thank a few special ones here. A big thanks to my daughter, Kendra Stearman, for helping me compile these articles and for naming this book. I would also like to thank my wife, Jane Alston Youmans, for her love and inspiration over the years and for helping me edit, and my friend Glenda Bell for her skillful editing.

Finally, I would like to thank the *Highlands Newspaper* in Highlands, North Carolina, in which many of these pieces were first published.

ABOUT THE AUTHOR
KENNY YOUMANS

Oftentimes wild ponies make the best horses.

I WAS BORN IN Swainsboro, Georgia, in 1941. The Youmans go back in that area to the early 1800s. My father grew up on a dairy farm during the Depression. If my grandmother had not been a schoolteacher, my grandfather would have lost his farm and the dairy. The Depression was hard. The land had been passed down within the family since about 1812. Among many things the land was a source of pride.

After WWII, my father, who was in the army, moved us to Pooler, Georgia. At that time, Pooler was a small town (population: 750) about ten miles out of Savannah on the west side. Highway 80 started in Tybee Island, Georgia, and went through the middle of Pooler all the way to Los Angeles, California. Highway 80 was the only road heading west at that time out of Savannah. Pooler was completely separate from Savannah. We had our own churches, drug store, movie theater, gas stations, hardware store, and elementary school.

We lived on two acres of land inside of Pooler. Our property included a barn. We owned a milk cow and a horse. We had a big vegetable garden. My father was a farmer at heart.

Starting in the second grade, I milked the cow twice a day. My pay was that I could sell two quarts a day for twenty cents a quart. That was $2.80 a week. Pretty good money in 1948 for a second grader. I remember buying a new Schwinn bike for sixty-three dollars at two dollars a week. Starting in the fifth grade, I sold *Grit* newspapers every Saturday—ten cents a paper. I probably made a couple of dollars a week.

Beginning in sixth grade, I was hired to sweep and clean the theater the day after the movies were shown. The movies were on Wednesday, Friday, and Saturday nights.

In the seventh grade, I would hitchhike to the Oglethorpe Speedway (somewhere between Savannah and Pooler) and sell soft drinks during the races. I don't remember if this was Saturday afternoon or Sunday afternoon. I do remember one of the most popular drivers was Moon Mullins. Today, I believe Moon Mullins writes articles on auto races.

During the summers and all holidays from 1947 to 1955, I lived with my grandparents on the family farm in Swainsboro. In 1947, my grandfather owned a dairy. The cows had to be milked twice a day. We would get started at about four o'clock every morning. The milk was delivered in town, door to door, seven days a week. Also, we had to collect the amount owed for the milk—usually once a month.

Finally my grandfather sold the dairy. Great move. Then he got into tobacco, cotton, beef cows, and hogs. I worked mostly in tobacco.

When I was in the eighth grade, we moved to Georgetown, South Carolina. We lived near the river where the paper mill was located. The barges would come by, loaded with pulpwood. Logs would fall off and drift to shore. A friend and I would gather the logs, put them in one pile, and sell them back to the paper mill.

We moved to Savannah in September 1955. During the summer that year, I would hitchhike from Skidaway Road to Bull Street. I worked as a bagger and stock boy at Cheatham's grocery store. It was located at the intersection of Bull and Washing Avenues. Cheatham's catered to a very exclusive area. In my mind everyone in that area was rich. When I delivered the groceries, of course I had to go to the back doors. Later, during high school, I dated the daughter of a family who lived in one of the homes in that area. It was the front door for me.

During my high school years, between sports, I sold ladies' shoes at Levy's Department Store and Butler's Shoe, and men's and boys' clothing at Levy's. Also during that time, I worked at Belk-Lindsey in the shopping center at Skidaway and Victory Drive selling men's and boy's clothing. At Belk-Lindsey, I worked with Johnny Mercer's niece. She was very good looking. However, she was a year older and paid me no attention.

After graduating from high school, I attended Abraham Baldwin Agriculture College (ABAC) in Tifton, Georgia, in my first two years of college. My father wanted me to major in agriculture. However, I had no interest in agriculture and majored in business.

ABAC was great for me. ABAC had record enrollment September 1959 with six hundred students. However, by the third quarter, attendance was down to three hundred. Many students were sons of farmers and had to help on the farm during spring and summer. I loved ABAC. I never went home except for summer and Christmas. I would go home many weekends with the sons of farmers and others from the small South Georgia towns. It was a perfect fit for me.

During my first two summers in college, I worked for the Seaboard Railroad as a brakeman and would travel from Savannah to Jacksonville or Savannah to Columbia. Sometimes it would take sixteen hours (rain or shine). We would spend the night in a boarding house and, after eight hours, repeat the trip back the next day.

After my first quarter at the University of Georgia (UBA), I dropped out and worked for the Central of Georgia Railroad for nine months. I started back at UGA in September of 1962. During my first quarter back, I had an *Atlanta Journal* paper route. That was a big mistake. In those days, the paper boy also had to collect, which I did at night to catch people home after their workdays. That was worse than delivering the paper. Half the time people wanted me to come back. Wally Butts (Georgia football coach) still owes me ten dollars. That's about it, except that one summer I ran a bar out on the Atlanta Highway.

After college, I went back to Savannah and lived with my parents, waiting to be accepted in military service. That was a great four months in Savannah. I sold men's clothing at Levy's Department Store. I knew everyone in Savannah I wanted to know. I lived at home, with no expenses and no responsibilities.

In January of 1965, I was sent to Fort Jackson in Columbia, South Carolina, for basic training. After three months of basic training, I was sent to Fayetteville, North Carolina, to become a member of the Eighty-Second Airborne Division. I went through jump school and eventually made eight jumps. This included one night jump, during which they dropped us off over some wooded mountain area somewhere in North Carolina. We had to survive for two weeks with rations. I promise, no one appreciates a hot shower more than I. I will never take a hot shower for granted. However, it is no comparison to the sacrifices of the servicemen and servicewomen risking their lives serving in Afghanistan or Iraq.

After my military commitment, I was hired by Burroughs Corporation in Savannah. Soon I transferred to Charleston, South Carolina. Burroughs was not a good fit for me. After seven months I resigned and moved to Atlanta. Probably half the students who graduate from UGA end up in Atlanta. Needless to say, I was happy to be with so many of my UGA friends. I took a job with Will Ross, a hospital supply company. However, after three months they sent me to Orlando, Florida. To be honest, I had never heard of Orlando, Florida, and certainly did not want to leave Atlanta. Luckily for me though, I had a blind date with Jane Alston the night before I left Atlanta. I think I fell in love before the night was over. It was hard to leave for Orlando the next day.

I wasn't too happy in Orlando at first. Every other weekend I would take off to Atlanta to see Jane. Interstate 75 wasn't even completed at that time. When I got to Perry, Georgia, I would have to take Highway 441 to Atlanta. It was a long trip. After eight months we were married. That was fifty-five years ago. We bought a place in Highlands, North Carolina, in 1998. That was a good decision. Highlands is special. All's well that ends well.

Kenny Youmans

A member of Kappa Alpha Order, University of Georgia

A member of the University of Georgia Gridiron Society

BIBLIOGRAPHY

1. Hughes, Langston. "Dreams." Poets.org. Accessed August 28, 2022. https://www.poets.org/poems/dreams.

2. Guest, Edgar A. "Don't Quit." Poemanalysis.com. Accessed August 28, 2022. https://www. poemanalysis.com/edgar-guest/dont-quit/.

3. Wikipedia. "Keep on the Sunny Side." Wikipedia. org. Accessed August 28, 2022. https://www. en.wikipedia.org/wiki/Keep_on_the_Sunny_ Side#lyrics.

4. Davis, Jimmie, and Charles Mitchell. "You Are My Sunshine." Lyrics.com. Accessed August 28, 2022. https://www.lyrics.com/lyric/17927930/ Bing+Crosby/You+Are+My+Sunshine.

5. "Songwriters and Music Legends of LaGrange." VisitLagrange.com. Accessed September 8, 2022. https://www.visitlagrange.com/songwriters-and-music-legends-of-lagrange/.

6. Pitts, William S. "The Church in the Wildwood." Public Domain.

7. "History." Littlebrownchurch.org. Accessed August 28, 2022. https://littlebrownchurch.org/the-church/history/.

8. The Ohio State University. "Harriett Beecher Stowe." ehistory.osu.edu. Accessed August 28, 2022. https://ehistory.osu.edu/articles/harriet-beecher-stowe-little-woman-who-wrote-book-started-great-war.

9. Edwards, Joe. "What's the most recorded song ever? 'Amazing grace.'" Updated November 10, 2010.

10. Associated Press. "Local Kansas Couple Adopts 'Fab Five' Siblings After Newspaper Story Spurs Worldwide Interest." Updated May 31, 2018. https://news.yahoo.com/local-kansas-coupleadopts-apos-000241401.html.

11. Soderlund Drugstore Museum. "History of the Soda Fountain." Accessed August 20, 2022. http://www.drugstoremuseum.com/soda-fountain/.

12. O'Neil, Darcy. "Soda Fountain History." Updated December 14, 2010. https://www.artofdrink.com/soda/chapter-1-introduction.

13. Britannica. "Woolworth Co." Encyclopedia Britannica. Updated May 26,

2014. https://www.britannica.com/topic/Woolworth-Co.

14. "Morrison's Cafeteria-1945." Encyclopedia of Alabama. Accessed August 20, 2022. http://www.encyclopediaofalabama.org/article/m951#:~:text=Morrison%27s%20Cafeteria%20was%20founded%20by%20J.%20A.%20Morrison,company%20and%20the%20discontinuation%20of%20the%20Morrison%27s%20name.

15. VisitSummerville.com, Accessed August 20, 2022. www.visitsummerville.com/sweet-tea-trail.

16. L, Mary. "History of Tea in the USA." TopicTea. Accessed August 20, 2022. http://topictea.com/blogs/tea-blog/history-of-tea-in-the-usa./

17. VisitSummerville.com, Accessed August 20, 2022. https://www.visitsummerville.com/sweet-tea-trail.

18 Girl Scouts of America. "Facts about Girl Scouts." Girl Scouts of America. Accessed August 20, 2022. https://www.girlscouts.org/en/footer/faq/facts.html.

19. Schmidt, Ann. "Girl Scout Cookies and what to know about the $800 million business." Fox Business. Updated March 12, 2020. https://www.foxbusiness.com/lifestyle/girl-scout-cookies-what-to-know.

20. Francis, Katie. "About Katie." *Katie Francis* (blog). Accessed August 20, 2022. https://katiefrancis. com/about-katie/.

21. Girl Scouts of America. Accessed August 20, 2022. https://www.girlscouts.org/en/footer/faq/facts.html https://www.girlscouts.org/content/dam/girlscouts-gsusa/forms-and-documents/about- girl-scouts/facts/GSUSA_facts_English_3-19.pdf.

22 Moore, Clement Clark. *The Night Before Christmas.* New York City: G.P. Putnam's Sons, 1998.

23. Wei-Haas, Maya. "Tired of Daylight Saving Time? These Places Are Trying to End It." Science. National Geographic, May 3, 2021. https://www.nationalgeographic.com/science/article/tired-of-daylight-saving-time-these-states-trying-to-end-clock-changes.

24. Nobel Lectures, Peace 1971-1980, Editor-in-Charge Tore Frängsmyr, Editor Irwin Abrams, World Scientific Publishing Co., Singapore, 1997.

25. History. "Mother's Day." History.com. Updated April 29, 2011. https://www.history.com/topics/holidays/mothers-day.

26. Krull, Kyle. "Wishing You and Yours a Blessed Thanksgiving." KyleKrull.com. Updated November 25, 2021. https://www.kylekrull. com/wishing-you-and-yours-a-blessed-thanksgiving/#:~:text=In%20the%20midst%20 of%20the%20conflict%20known%20as,all%20 Americans%20on%20the%20last%20Thu-rsday%20of%20November.

27. Wikipedia. "Thanksgiving" Wikipedia.org. Accessed August 25, 2022. https://en.wikipedia.org/wiki/ Thanksgiving#In_the_United_States.

28. Anonymous. "At Grandma's House." Loving2Learn. com. Accessed October 13, 2022. http://www. loving2learn.com/Activities/Thanksgiving/ ThanksgivingPoems/AtGrandmasHouse. aspx Anonymous. "At Grandma's House." DiscoverPoetry.com. Accessed August 25, 2022. https://discoverpoetry.com/poems/turkey-poems/.

29. Landers, Ann. "Signed the Rotten Kid." *The Best of Ann Landers: Her Favorite Letters of All Time.* New York, NY: Fawcett Columbine, 1997.

30. Wikipedia. "Phyllis Diller." Wikipedia.org. Accessed August 25, 2022. https://en.wikipedia.org/wiki/ Phyllis_Diller.

31. Bernstein, Elizabeth. "Finding Hope When Everything Feels Hopeless." *The Wall Street Journal*. October 27, 2020.

32. Hope Grows. "Why is hope so important?" HopeGrows.com. Accessed August 25, 2022. https://hopegrows.net/news/why-is-hope-so-important.

33. Cino, Charles A. "Now You've Recovered." Familyfriendpoems.com. Accessed September 7, 2022. https://www.familyfriendpoems.com/poem/now-youve-recovered.

34. Campus Crusade for Christ. www.cru.org. Accessed September 7, 2022. https://cru.org/

35. Wikipedia.org. "The Power of Positive Thinking." wikipedia.org. Accessed August 25, 2022. https://en.wikipedia.org/wiki/The_Power_of_Positive_Thinking.

36. Hintz, Eric S. "Benjamin Franklin's Inventions." Smithsonian. Updated December 16, 2016. https://invention.si.edu/benjamin-franklin-sinventions#:~:text=As%20a%20scientist%2C%20he%20was%20a%20major%20figure,including%20%E2%80%9Cbattery%2C%E2%80%9D%20%E2%80%9Cpositive%E2%80%9D%20and%20%E2%80%9Cnegative%2C%E2%80%9D%20%E2%80%9Cconductor%2C%E2%80%9D%20and%20%E2%80%9Cdischarge.%E2%80%9D.

37. Wikipedia. "Poor Richard's Almanack." Wikipedia.org. Accessed August 25, 2022. https://en.wikipedia.org/wiki/Poor_Richard%27s_Almanack.

38. Homemade Gifts Made Easy. "30 Happy Father's Day Poems." Homemadegiftsmadeeasy.com. Updated May 31, 2021. https://www.homemade-gifts-made-easy.com/fathers-day-poems.html.

39. Young, Neely. *Georgia Made: The Most Important Figures Who Shaped the State in the Twentieth Century.* Charleston: The History Press, 2021.

40. "Jesus Loves Me This I Know." bibilium.com. Accessed September 8, 2022.

    https://bibilium.com/jesus-loves-me-this-i-know-jesus-loves-me-song/.

41. Warner, Anna B., 1860 v. 2-3 by David R. McGuire ref. by William B. Bradbury, 1862.

42. Meghan. "The History of the Valentines Day Card." History Cooperative. Updated February 14, 2017. Accessed September 8, 2022. https://historycooperative.org/history-valentines-day-card/.

43. Mass Moments. "First American Made Valentines Sold." MassMoments.org. Accessed August 25, 2022. https://www.massmoments.org/moment-details/first-american-made-valentines-sold.html.

44. Balancing Everything. "Valentine's Day Sales Statistics." Balancingeverything.com. Accessed September 7, 2022. https://balancingeverything.com/valentines-day-sales-Statistics/.

45. Young, Neely. *Georgia Made: The Most Important Figures Who Shaped the State in the Twentieth Century.* Charleston: The History Press, 2021.

46. All About History. "Origin of the Word Easter." allabouthistory.com. Accessed August 25, 2022. https://www.allabouthistory.org/origin-of-the-word-easter-faq.htm.

47. History. "Easter 2022." History.com. Updated April 7, 2022. https://www.history.com/topics/holidays/history-of-easter.

48. History. "Easter 2022." History.com. Updated April 7, 2022.

https://www.history.com/topics/holidays/history-of-easter.

49. Autry, Gene, Steve Nelson, and Jack Rollins. "Here Comes Peter Cottontail." Decca Records, 1950.

50. Unknown

51. Wikipedia. "How to Win Friends and Influence People." Wikipedia.org. Accessed August 25, 2022. https://en.wikipedia.org/wiki/How_to_Win_Friends_and_Influence_People.

52. Carnegie, Dale. *How to Win Friends and Influence People*. New York: Simon and Schuster, 1936.

53. Rios, Valerie S. "The Perfect Friend." Updated October 2007. https://www.familyfriendpoems.com/poem/greeting-card-friendship-poem.

54. Trivia Library. "Origins of Sayings." TriviaLibrary.com. Accessed August 25, 2022. https://trivia-library.com/b/origins-of-sayings-laugh-and-the-world-laughs-with-you.htm.

55. Divine You. "8 Health Benefits of Smiling Proven by Science." DivineYouWellness.com. Accessed August 25, 2022. https://divineyouwellness.com/blog/benefits-of-smiling/#:~:text=%208%20Health%20Benefits%20of%20Smiling%20%201,when%20a%20person%20smiles.%20Subsequently%2C%20the...%20More%20.

56. Poole, William C. "What a Smile Will Do." Public domain.

57. Gaba, Sherry. "Fame, Mania and Depression: The Hidden Link." BeliefNet.com. Accessed August 25, 2022. https://www.beliefnet.com/columnists/thecelebritytherapist/2013/10/fame-mania-and-depression-the-hiddenlink.html#:~:text=In%20a%20very%20recent%20study%20published%20in%202013%2C,a%20significant%20number%20that%20have%20it%20in%20common.

58. Historic Boalsburg. "Memorial Day." HistoricBoalsburg.com. Accessed August 25, 2022. https://historicboalsburg.com/things-to-do/memorial-day/.

59. History Net. "The Battle of Gettysburg: Facts & Info About a Turning Point in the Civil War." Historynet.com. Accessed August 2, 2022. https://www.historynet.com/battle-of-Gettysburg/.

60. Associated Press. "A timeline of the US military presence in Afghanistan." APNews.com. Updated September 8, 2019. https://apnews.com/article/fd2ec2085b0b4fd3ae0a3b03c6de9478.

61. Cohen, Michelle. "Macy's fireworks by the numbers." Pyrospec.com. June 29, 2018. https://www.pyrospec.com/macys-2018-by-the-numbers/#:~:text=More%20fun%20facts%20The%20first%20big%20Macy%E2%80%99s%20fireworks,Walt%20Disney%20Company%20to%20celebrate%20the%20nation%E2%80%99s%20Bicentennial.

62. NBWA. "Industry Fast Facts." NBWA.org. Accessed August 25, 2022. https://www.nbwa.org/resources/industry-fast-facts.

63. Wikipedia. "Joey Chestnut." Wikipedia.org. Accessed August 25, 2022. https://en.wikipedia.org/wiki/Joey_Chestnut.

64. Miller, Kori D. "14 Health Benefits of Practicing Gratitude According to Science." PositivePsychology.com. Updated June 18, 2019. https://positivepsychology.com/benefits-of-gratitude/#benefits.

65. Schor, Jacob. "Gratitude Diary Improves Mood in Suicidal Inpatients." Natural Medicine Journal. Updated September 4, 2019. https://www.naturalmedicinejournal.com/journal/gratitude-diary-improves-mood-suicidal-inpatients.

66. Anderson, Erika. "How Feeling Grateful Can Make You More Successful." Forbes.com. Updated November 27, 2013. https://www.forbes.com/sites/erikaandersen/2013/11/27/how-feeling-grateful-can-make-you-more-successful/?sh=1394d6312de7.

67 Brown, Joshua, and Joel Wong. "How Gratitude Changes You and Your Brain." GreaterGoodMagazine.com. Updated June 6, 2017. https://greatergood.berkeley.edu/article/item/how_gratitude_changes_you_and_your_brain.

68. Michael, Moina. "We Shall Keep The Faith." Wikipedia.org. Accessed August 25, 2022. https://en.wikipedia.org/wiki/We_Shall_Keep_the_Faith.

69. Hamilton, Robert Browing. "I Walked a Mile with Pleasure." Goodreads.com. Accessed October 13, 2022. https://www.goodreads.com/quotes/289683-i-walked-a-mile-with-pleasure-she-chatted-all-the

70. Unknown

71. Wikipedia. "I Will Always Love You." Wikipedia.org. Accessed August 28, 2022. https://en.wikipedia.org/wiki/I_Will_Always_Love_You

CPSIA information can be obtained
at www.ICGtesting.com
Printed in the USA
BVHW071845151222
654333BV00013B/781

9 798885 908894